# DES
# INTO SILENCE

# DESCENT INTO SILENCE

Cawthorne's Forgotten Tragedy

## David Hinchliffe

Scratching Shed Publishing Ltd

Cover illustration: Harry Malkin

Typeset in Warnock Pro Semi Bold and Palatino
Printed and bound in the United Kingdom by

Unit 600, Fareham Reach, Fareham Road
Gosport, Hampshire, PO13 0FW

This book is in memory of my collier ancestors,
of whom I am extremely proud

# Contents

# Victims of
# 1821 Norcroft Pit Disaster

Thomas Blackburn, aged 16.

Benjamin Eyre, aged 10.

Charles Eyre, aged 16.

Robert Eyre, aged 12.

Charles Forden, aged 8.

John Handfirth, aged 45.

John Hinchliffe, aged 8.

John Townend, aged 13.

Thomas Townend, aged 23.

Richard Watson, aged 47.

# Foreword

COALMINE DISASTERS devastated the lives of families and communities, no more so than from the 1850s and '60s, at the height of Queen Victoria's reign. Within a day or two, households throughout the land, mainly through local newspapers, got detailed 'first-hand' information about the latest coalfield calamity.

Our knowledge and understanding of earlier times, when mining was much smaller in scale and often found on small country estates, is far sketchier. Records then were relatively scarce, there were no mines inspectors to report findings, no proper public inquiries and relatively few, easily accessible newspapers.

Furthermore, over the course of time, old pits soon became lost landscape features, extremely difficult to identify today, even with reference to maps and modern technology.

The remarkable feature of David Hinchliffe's book lies in the way he has not only managed to overcome those research problems, but actually enhanced our knowledge and appreciation of some of the wider aspects of the Norcroft disaster.

## Descent into Silence

This, I feel sure, has been driven by his personal family connection to one of the disaster victims, eight-year-old John Hinchliffe. Entwined is the way he also applies an historian's skill to place the boy miner and his fellows, indeed the very mine itself, in context – as a place of work and way of life so dependent on a dominant landed family.

In 1821, rural communities such as Cawthorne and Silkstone had no proper support mechanisms to help the bereaved families of the men, women, boys and girls who were killed and maimed in pits. It was a situation that changed little until the amalgamation of the miners' unions into a powerful, single body, the National Union of Mineworkers, in 1945, and the nationalisation of the coal industry two years later.

I cannot help think now, after 200 years, there has been no better way of describing and explaining the Norcroft disaster to present and future generations than in reading David's insightful book. It is a very tragic story but not without its 'advantages', its social messages, its long-term implications.

By the latter I mean that David's contribution will now enable teachers and schoolchildren –– as well as the wider public – to be provided with a balanced, well researched account of what happened on that terrible May morning when the winding 'rope' snapped and boys and men plunged in darkness to the bottom of the shaft.

What a hellish experience it must have been. I feel sure, also, that this study will serve as an exemplar for others to model and aspire to when researching early colliery disasters.

*Brian Elliott*
*Author and mining historian*

# Preface

David Hinchliffe

IT IS my sincere hope that this book will act as an encouragement to others to allow genealogical study to lead them into researching wider aspects of social history as it has impacted upon their own ancestors. It is a fact that my encounter with the Norcroft story arises directly from the involvement of my own family with what happened in 1821. Family historians will discover ancestral connections with other significant events which remain largely or completely unrecorded but should be a part of our wider understanding of what happened in the past, often in communities whose stories are usually ignored.

The background research which book draws together began as a purely genealogical project undertaken by my wife, Julia, and myself, many years ago. A considerable amount of the information contained in it has been obtained through direct access to primary sources which are fully referenced wherever possible. Initial access to parish records relating to Norcroft and the wider Cawthorne and Silkstone areas occurred when it was possible to personally handle them. Such access is now, quite rightly, usually done on microfiche machines which allow perusal of the originals in a way which avoids their wear and tear. Much of the book's research has been undertaken in this way but a good deal of it has relied upon transcriptions of original records which are available in published record series and on-line via *FamilySearch* or subscription services which can, in some areas, be accessed through local library and archive services. Most local family history societies publish detailed parish records for their area, and I have found these invaluable with this project although there can be errors during transcription just as there are, quite obviously sometimes, with the original records.

While I have endeavoured to include detailed references to as many sources as possible it was impractical to list all those obtained from parish registers but these will be clear from the text. I am conscious that such registers usually only include male occupations within their entries, with the result that the role of women and girls during the period covered is less apparent. Similarly, local census returns during the 19th century more often recorded the work undertaken by men. The pursuit, primarily, of the male lines of those involved in this story also tells an incomplete history. Their maternal ancestry needs to be investigated to ensure a more comprehensive account and what may be seen as the masculine focus of this story does not in any way underestimate the way so many women and girls suffered appallingly at this time. The deaths during and around childbirth, alone, are testimony to this.

As a member of a local history society, I would also want to acknowledge the importance of the information gained from often largely unheralded local groups engaged in the study of their own communities and individuals who have immense local knowledge. As I have found on a number of occasions, a walk around the Banks, Norcroft and Cawthorne areas with those who live, or have lived, in the area can significantly enhance an understanding of its local history which would otherwise rely on published sources.

Finally, in an effort to ensure that this book's publication coincides with the Norcroft disaster's bi-centenary, it ought to be noted that much of the research undertaken has been done during the Covid pandemic when there have frequently been severe restrictions on access to local authority-held archive materials. Ideally, I would have liked to revisit a number of the primary sources quoted in the book to verify my interpretation of their significance. This has simply not been possible and, as a consequence, I would urge some caution in their use without further validation.

I regard this book as just an introduction to what was happening in the Cawthorne and Silkstone areas during this fascinating time in our history. I am told that Dr. Samuel Johnson once said, "A writer only starts a book. A reader finishes it." I genuinely hope there might be others who will complete this story, correct any errors in my research and fill in some of the many gaps I will have missed.

*David Hinchliffe*
*May 2021*

Cawthorne burials register, April/May, 1821    *Barnsley MBC*

# 1.

# Facing Pages

THE YEAR of 1821 was one of great sadness in the West Riding village of Cawthorne, near Barnsley. The local squire, a leading figure in the community and former MP, Sir Walter Spencer-Stanhope of nearby Cannon Hall, had breathed his last in the seventy-third year of his life. He was buried at All Saints Church, Cawthorne, amid much public mourning, on April 21, 1821. A marble memorial tablet, originally under the East Window of his family's burial chapel within the church, set out a detailed tribute to his life, *as reproduced overleaf*.

The entry for Spencer-Stanhope's death in the burials section of Cawthorne Parish register, *pictured left*, is far less embellished, recording merely his name, address of Cannon Hall and age at passing, alongside the details of those interred at Cawthorne around the same time. On the facing page, exactly opposite his entry, and dated just over a month later, is the record of the burial of an eight-year-old boy, John Hinchliffe, of Norcroft. Immediately above and below this

*Here rest the remains*

*Of*

**WALTER SPENCER STANHOPE esquire**

*Born on the 4th day of February, 1749,*
*Died on the 4th day of April, 1821.*

*From his paternal and maternal uncles, John Stanhope, of*
*Horseforth Hall, and John Spencer, of Cannon Hall, esquires,*
*he inherited the estates and united the names of both families.*

*He married Mary Winefred, sole daughter and heiress of*
*Wingate Pulleine, of Carleton Hall, esquire, by whom he had*
*fifteen children; twelve, with their surviving Parent,*
*are left to revere his memory and lament his loss;*

*By nature and education endowed with every quality which*
*befitted his station, he was esteemed in public*
*and beloved in private life.*

*In Parliament, where he faithfully discharged his duty for a space*
*of nearly 40 years his conduct was ever upright and consistent,*
*and his vote prompted by an ardent zeal*
*for the interest of his country.*

*In the Militia of his county, and in the Yeomanry of his district,*
*he bore arms in her defence, and at a season of great national*
*alarm, as commandant of the Volunteers of the Wapentake,*
*he was amongst the foremost to face the dangers*
*and repel the threats of invasion.*

*A pious and benevolent Christian, a loyal and patriotic subject,*
*a tender relation, and a steadfast friend, he blended the*
*accomplishments, concentrated the worth, and exemplified the*
*character, of an English country gentleman, bequeathing to his*
*descendants at the close of a useful life the richest of all legacies,*
*a virtuous example.*[1]

entry are noted the names of four other children also interred on the same day and killed with him in a pit accident on land owned by the Spencer-Stanhope family. It is difficult to avoid the conclusion that adjacent entries for posterity in these local parish records were perhaps all Sir Walter and these boys ever had in common.

Certainly, the circumstances of their deaths differed markedly. While the children had plunged almost 120 feet down a pit shaft, Spencer-Stanhope had passed away peacefully at his London 'town house' in Langham Place, close to what are now the capital's main studios of the BBC. His funeral was meticulously planned, with an "Order of Procession"[2] setting out in considerable detail the manner in which the deceased was to be taken on his final journey from Cannon Hall to All Saints Church in nearby Cawthorne.

At its head were some of his very many tenants on horseback, then others on foot. The hearse carrying his body had feathers on it and there were feathers and velvet on the six horses pulling it. The four horses drawing the mourning coach also had feathers and velvet. It contained the "Chief Mourners", noted as John Spencer-Stanhope, Esq., William Roddam, Esq, The Rev. Charles Spencer-Stanhope and Philip Spencer-Stanhope, Esq.

Four other mourning coaches followed with other relatives and close acquaintances, all males, the last containing senior estate employees, such as Spencer-Stanhope's longstanding agent, John Howson. Behind them, in a chaise and pair, was the officiating minister, The Reverend J. P. Buce.

Pulled by four horses, after Rev. Buce, came Sir Walter Spencer-Stanhope's own carriage – "Empty. Blinds drawn up" – and two servants behind with "Mourning Scarves, Gloves and Hatbands." Five other carriages followed, containing family members of the male mourners who had gone before.

The precise arrangements for the day involved Rev. Buce leaving the procession once it reached "The Lodges in Tivy Dale" and passing on ahead in order that he might be ready to receive the coffin on its arrival at the Church. The eight bearers of the pall would all appear to have been on horseback as the Order bid them "please to dismount in such time that they may be in attendance at the Hearse to fall into their places at the Pall on the corps (sic) being removed out of the Hearse." They included "Mr. Thorp" and "Mr. West", of Banks Hall and Lower Norcroft respectively. Either it was the age or infirmity of the bearers or concern over their burden which led to an additional safeguard in case of difficulties. According to the Order "Not more than six under-bearers…(were) to be in attendance lest the weight should be too much…"

The Cannon Hall accounts for 1821 make clear the funeral that Spring day was, indeed, a very significant event. The house's servants were provided with hats made especially for the occasion by Rebecca Hood at a cost of 11s. 3d. Martha Wood received 8s. for making them gowns. Preparing Cawthorne Church to receive the deceased's remains that April had involved paying George Ibbotson Taylor 11s. Messrs. Wilcock and Houson's (sic) expenses in respect of the funeral amounted to £7.1s.6d. and 13s.1 1/2d respectively, while Joseph Broadbent's came to £2.10s.0d. George Greenwood and his assistant were paid 15s.0d for "making a grave in Cawthorne Church." And, when the year of his death was drawing to an end, the significant sum of £86.10s.6d. "for mourning (was) given to the servants" of Sir Walter, probably marking the formal end of the grieving period.

## Facing Pages

We know a great deal less about the final journeys of those on the facing page of the burials register. With, no doubt, a good deal less ceremonial, on May 25, 1821 – just over a month after Spencer-Stanhope's death – along with another boy aged eight, and three more aged ten, twelve and sixteen, John Hinchliffe was being lowered into an unmarked grave, also at All Saints Church, Cawthorne. A brief, passing mention of their funerals in a Barnsley newspaper over sixty years later suggests that good numbers had followed the deceased to their final resting place[3], but even just their extended families and immediate neighbours would have constituted a sizeable assembly. Their simple coffins had been put together at Norcroft, near to where they had been killed two days earlier in the pit shaft plunge. Five others, including a second sixteen-year-old boy, also died, with another of the same age very seriously injured. The deceased received no obituaries and, until very recent times, have been almost totally forgotten.

A sketch of Cannon Hall from 1821 *Barnsley MBC*

# 2.

# Selective Histories

I RECALL being particularly struck by reading in a newspaper article not long ago, the suggestion that "Our version of the American dream is a perverse heritage myth that the lives of a tiny, rich minority can tell a shared national story."[4] It very much corresponded with my own perception that the recorded histories – of this country and many others – frequently tend to offer a rather partial account of the times they cover, reflecting so very often, first and foremost, the lives of the propertied and powerful. It is – again and again – their diaries, memoirs and estate accounts which shape our attempts to understand the past, just occasionally referring almost in passing to the provision of labour and service by those who have clearly been born into considerably less advantage.

Visitors flock in their thousands to Cawthorne to visit Cannon Hall, its estate and farm, where the Spencer-Stanhope story endures amid country house splendours. It is difficult not to be struck by the likes of its dining room, drawing room, ballroom and library, rare items of furniture and the picture displays. Most will enjoy any time spent there but, if an appreciation of the Hall's past is part of their purpose, being taken in any way beyond a neat 'Downton Abbey' type account of the history is most unlikely. But, as with every establishment of its nature and age, Cannon Hall has a past which belies the cosy gentility so attractive to those drawn to a nostalgic simplicity, uncomplicated by the rights and wrongs of what was going on at any particular time. I think it is fair to say that, long before I became aware of my past family ties with the area, I too had enjoyed this escapism and the perception, during visits, of being at what had perhaps been some sort of eighteenth and nineteenth century rural idyll.

It would be completely wrong to single out Cannon Hall for particular criticism over offering an incomplete story to the visitor, as the same comment might be made about any number of country seats in Yorkshire and further afield. We know now that a good few had connections, for example, with the slave trade although there cannot be very many which have actually had a slave trading ship named after it.

Interestingly, the most common story linking Cannon Hall to slavery is the putative friendship between the abolitionist MP, William Wilberforce and Sir Walter Spencer-Stanhope, when he was also an MP. Sir Walter's niece, Anna Maria Wilhelmina Stirling, gives the clear impression in her *Annals of a Country House* memoir[5], that Wilberforce was a very regular visitor to Cannon Hall, although this is not the picture gained from correspondence within the Spencer-Stanhope family archives. In fact, by contrast, these records offer considerable detail of the Spencer family's ownership and use of the sloop *Cannon Hall* for slave transportation and their having insurance for this trade between the years 1754-1758.[6]

My guidebook to what is nowadays called a "Country House Museum" advises that Cannon Hall had passed around this time from William Spencer to his eldest son, John, who was soon to begin landscaping the grounds and altering the house.[7] The family papers concerning John's younger brother, Benjamin Spencer, give insights into what we now recognise as a shameful episode of our history which, in all its detail, perhaps ought now to be more evident to the visiting Cannon Hall public. Spencer had extensive contact with a slave trader named Charles Quinsac who was based at what the British knew as St. James' Fort on the River Gambia, in West Africa, and acted as Secretary to the Committee of Merchants trading to Africa. One letter from him, in late 1755, detailed how, during a voyage from Gambia, a total of twenty-three slaves and two sailors had died.[8] Another deposition in Antigua around the same time outlined how during another voyage from West Africa carrying twenty-five slaves on board, seven of them had died, with two apparently killing themselves.[9] During February of the following year some correspondence refers to the sale of "ten sickly slaves" on behalf of Benjamin Spencer[10] and one invoice concerning the on-board merchandise details that, in addition to the slaves being carried, there was also gold and elephants' teeth.[11]

With a greater recent awareness of the – often inappropriate – commemoration, through statues and memorials of individuals with similar past connections, it may well be that Cannon Hall will, in the near future, offer a rather broader picture of its past than is currently the case. When and if this happens, it is to be hoped that alongside such chapters in its history as the slave trade, there will as well be an attempt to give more consideration to the great mass of wholly anonymous local folk who made their – often humble – contributions towards enabling such as the Spencer-Stanhopes to live in considerable style and comfort.

Most visitors coming to the Hall and many local residents, continue to be completely unaware of the stories of those who, in the quite recent past, lived out their lives in this same neighbourhood, frequently facing a daily struggle to survive. Most are oblivious to the fact that, not very long ago, the fires of such splendidly ornate mansions burned coal which children working underground nearby helped to produce. The surviving accounts of the Spencer-Stanhope household show that the (until recently) totally forgotten young victims of this 1821 tragedy most likely met their deaths playing minor, but crucially important roles, in extracting the local coal which would have heated the numerous hearths of Cannon Hall.[12] They list regular payments by the Spencer-Stanhopes of quite significant amounts of money for coal to Samuel Thorp, the entrepreneur responsible at the time for working several local pits, including those at Norcroft.

Two centuries on, this book attempts to offer some record of the lives of the disaster victims, their families, their small community, and of the circumstances in which those lives were tragically lost.

# 3.

# Curious Connections

ONE OF my most precious material possessions is a photograph of my Hinchliffe family, taken on the Golden Wedding of my great-grandparents, Benjamin and Eliza, at their home in Elsicker Lane, Warmfield, near Wakefield, during 1903. It was given to me by a very elderly relative – my father's cousin – who I had neither known about nor met until, quite a number of years ago, Julia and I had started on the infinite journey towards uncovering our family histories. The advice to all genealogists in the embryonic stage of their research about speaking to senior family members was to prove particularly fruitful.

'Auntie' May Ellis, as we knew her, has been wonderfully remembered by my cousin, Anne Wilkinson, as "small in height, bright and busy, with sharp wits and a quick but kind tongue".[13] She was, in fact, not actually our aunt but, as the niece of our grandfather, presumably a second cousin. This remarkable woman was on that photograph as a

**Hinchliffe family photograph from 1903.** Benjamin Hinchliffe is seated in the centre and May Ellis (*née Ladlow*) is standing immediately behind Benjamin's wife, Eliza. Their son, Oliver, is standing on the right of the photograph, alongside his brother Jack. Ethel Hinchliffe (*née Woodhead*) is on the back row, slightly to the right, behind May Ellis　　　　　　　　　　　　　*David Hinchliffe*

---

thirteen- year-old girl, and, in giving me a copy of it, was able to tell me stories about each and every member of the family who was featured. She brought the sparsest details of their identity – which we had by then obtained from census returns and parish registers – to vivid life. Individuality and personality were added to what had been just names, together with odd bits of gossip delivered with a mischievous smile. Not only had my great-uncle, Jack Hinchliffe, played for Wakefield Trinity before the Northern Union split between the rugby codes in 1895 but, unusually for someone involved in the most robust of sports, he had also been an accomplished violinist.

There was one particularly tall and well-dressed gentleman in the photograph who stood out among the predominantly stocky, modestly clad colliers and labourers constituting my kinsmen. Bates Newsome came from what might have been viewed as slightly grander stock in Morley, marrying into the family, and had posed for the picture wearing an obviously expensive, broad-brimmed trilby hat. Auntie May's particular recollection of him has remained with me. On cold winter's days he had the unusual habit of placing his hat inside the oven compartment of the household's coal-burning range to warm it, before placing it on his head.

And, in a matter-of-fact sort of way she pointed out how, like so many families of that period, ours was also affected by the horrors of the First World War. One of the four small boys looking up at the camera from the front row was one of the thousands coming from Yorkshire's West Riding alone who succumbed in the terrible slaughter.

Born May Ladlow, also in Warmfield on 19 May 1890, she had married James Edward Ellis, a railway man, and was widowed living in an elderly person's bungalow in Well Hill Grove, Royston, near Barnsley, when we talked towards the end of the 1980s. Sometime later, when living independently had become more difficult, Auntie May moved into what was then the Banks Hall residential care home, a few miles to the west of Royston, off Woolstock Lane, Cawthorne. One evening, during the February before her forthcoming hundredth birthday, I had a detailed discussion in the House of Commons with Eric Illsley and Allen McKay, then the MPs for the Royston and Cawthorne areas respectively, about the three of us jointly visiting her on her approaching special day. However, on the very same evening of our dialogue on phoning home, I learned that Auntie May had passed away during the previous day. She died of what some used to term 'the old people's friend' – broncho-pneumonia – just three months and fifteen days before reaching her centenary.

I knew that she had been aware of some past family connections with Cawthorne, as she had the vaguest recollection of coming from Warmfield to visit family or friends in the area on a horse and trap while still a very small girl. But Auntie May had not the least idea of any of the fateful events impacting upon her own family earlier in the century in which she was born, just a few hundred yards away from where she ended her days. In particular, she knew nothing of the circumstances of the tragic death of an eight-year-old boy – most likely her great-uncle John – down a pit just a few minutes' walk away from where she was living. Neither was she aware of the fact that he had been involved in producing coal for the man who lived at the time in the very house where she was spending her final days – Banks Hall.

The mining of that coal had begun in earnest in the locality after the linking of the Barnsley Canal at Barnby, near Cawthorne, to the Aire and Calder navigation in Wakefield in 1802. Auntie May probably never saw the coal barges depart from alongside the old Jolly Sailor public house in Barnby Basin, heading north with their loads. But she would certainly have known the house which bargees coming from the Calder passed going in the opposite direction through the second and third locks at the other end of the canal in

**Undated oil painting** by Oliver Hinchliffe of the Barnsley Canal entering the River Calder at Heath Lock, near Wakefield. The image portrayed may not have been entirely accurate, but Dame Mary Bolles's water tower and well is clearly featured on the left.

*David Hinchliffe*

Wakefield, before they entered the two-mile pound leading to the twelve lock Walton flight. She would also most likely have been present there – at Hough Cottage, Agbrigg[14] – on Christmas Day 1900, when Ethel Woodhead left her childhood home to marry May's uncle, Oliver Hinchliffe, at nearby Crofton Church. Ethel's father, Martin, and grandfather, Thomas, were key contributors to the functioning of the waterway which directly linked the parish where May's life had begun to the one where she would spend her final days. Both men had built and repaired the boats carrying the coal along the canal which had been the lifeblood of Cawthorne's industrial revolution. On my only visit to the cottage during the 1990s, when its longstanding Lancaster family occupants were still there, it was still possible to see a wall-papered over gap in the outside wall through which the bargees used to settle up what they owed.

Perhaps an even more extraordinary connection to the location of this story stems from Julia, also pursuing her own ancestry and researching her paternal grandmother's Greaves family. Born in Scotland, while her father was serving in the Royal Navy on the Clyde, Julia grew up in his home area of North Wales and had no knowledge whatsoever of any Yorkshire connections. But tracing their male line back via Liverpool, Manchester and Glossop in Derbyshire, she found that her great-grandfather, Jonathan Greaves – who had been born at Langsett, near Penistone – was actually living in Cawthorne on September 27, 1812, when he had married Mary Marshall in the local church. He is later recorded as living at Cawthorne Lane, with Greaves also noted as residing at Bentcliff Hill and Pease Grove, off South Lane, Cawthorne, as well as Hill House, close to Norcroft. The family's presence in the area at the time may well have been marked by some land known locally as 'Greaves Fold'[15]. Incredibly, this was located at Upper Norcroft, where Robert Greaves – most likely Jonathan's brother – was living not long after the 1821 tragedy.[16]

# 4

# Earth's Immeasurable Surprise

THE AWESOME changes in nature which signal the arrival of Spring are summed up wonderfully in Philip Larkin's poem, *First Sight*, as "Earth's immeasurable surprise." In many respects, the month of May represents the remarkable consolidation of that, so very welcome, seasonal advance. But the Cawthorne and Silkstone of May 1821 would have seen a very different environment from that of today. Travelling along the – nowadays fairly quiet and pleasant Silkstone Lane – would back then have brought the wayfarer alongside a powerhouse of human activity, with a landscape scarred by intense industrial exploitation. The sights would have been accompanied by the clatter of the wagonway and its branches transporting coal from the various pits along the way from Silkstone to the canal at Barnby Basin.

The clean air ushered in by smokeless zones was a long way off and, surrounded by mounds of slag and waste, the Norcroft cottages would lie within a pervading

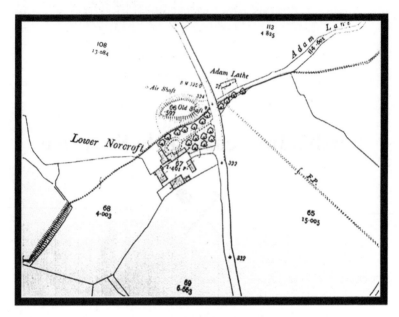

A map of Lower Norcroft, with adjacent wagonway          *J. Ritchie*

atmosphere of smoke from wood and coal fires and the steam engine running at Lower Norcroft Colliery. The outside privies, serving a total of almost twenty families, would have become even more pungent as the temperature rose. Nevertheless, the arrival of longer days and the pleasant, milder weather would, undoubtedly, have been welcomed after the dark harshness of winter. Set alongside the joys of nature's beauty again coming to life, the tragedy that was to befall the families of those working at the Norcroft pit seems extraordinarily untimely.

A key theme of this book is the extent to which the lives of the local gentry of the Cawthorne area at this time are extensively chronicled, often in considerable detail, while the day-to-day, lifelong struggles of the majority of the population have received scant regard. Nowhere is this more markedly illustrated than with the lamentable record of exactly what happened on 23 May 1821.

In terms of contemporary news report, we are reliant upon the very briefest of accounts in the *Leeds Intelligencer*, the forerunner of the *Yorkshire Post* newspaper, on 26 May 1821.[17] Its article offered just very basic detail that, on the previous Wednesday morning, "a melancholy accident occurred at a colliery at Silkston, (sic) near Barnsley." It outlined how, "Between nine and ten o'clock, eleven men employed in that colliery, were ascending from one of the pits, and after having nearly reached the top, the brig gave way, and the chain breaking, the whole were unfortunately precipitated to the bottom, a depth of nearly sixty yards." The report concluded that, "Six of them were killed, and the remainder so dreadfully injured, as to leave but little hopes of their recovery."[18] Three days later, in its edition of 29 May, the *Iris Sheffield Advertiser* carried a similar report.[19] Significantly, while the *Leeds Intelligencer* noted that, "Most of the unfortunate sufferers have left families,"[20] it referred to all the victims as being men. No mention was made in either of the reports that half the fatalities involved children, with two as young as just eight.

To gain some appreciation of the very real human consequences of the disaster, it is extremely fortunate that a contemporaneous memoir exists in the form of a letter written by an individual who was in the area at the time, and privy to the full extent of its aftermath. Jeremiah Gilbert was a 31-year-old Primitive Methodist preacher who sent a detailed written account about what happened shortly afterwards to his mother. He was the son of John and Elizabeth Gilbert, born in Caunton, Nottinghamshire in 1789 and baptised into the Anglican faith that year at the local St.

## Descent into Silence

Andrew's Church. Gilbert was part of a sizeable band of evangelistic preachers visiting parishes like Cawthorne and Silkstone around this time. Depicting the phenomenon, E.P. Thompson suggested that, "Through the streets of (Napoleonic) war-time and post-war England went the revivalist missionaries, crying out: 'Turn to the Lord and seek salvation.'"[21] Some established permanent roots in the area. Cawthorne's neighbouring parish of Darton, for example, saw John Pearson of Gainsborough described as an "Itinerant preacher in the late Mr Wesley's Connection" at his marriage there in 1814 to Sarah Thorp.

Gilbert's missionary work had taken him north from Nottinghamshire in 1819 to the Sheffield area, preaching at various points on the way including Bolsover where, on 18 May, he found himself arrested along with several supporters and held in the Round House, the town lock-up. A local clergyman was a key witness pressing the case against Gilbert but magistrates later released him. During June of the following year he noted in his journals that during the previous fifteen months he had found himself in front of magistrates as a result of preaching at least half-a-dozen times. He wrote, "…but I have never lost anything but pride, shame, unbelief, hardness of heart, the fear of men, love of the world and prejudice of mind. I have always come out of prison more pure than I went in."[22]

While Wesleyan Methodism has been described as a religion *for* the poor, Primitive Methodism is defined as a religion *of* the poor[23] and, as such, finding Gilbert – a self-proclaimed Ranter[24] – dwelling among the colliers of Silkstone and Cawthorne is consistent with the evangelism of his faith. His journals further indicate that he clearly spent much of his time travelling, preaching with obvious passion in an effort to convert non-believers to his brand of the

Wolfstone Heights, near Holmfirth                    *David Hinchliffe*

Christian faith. He records in some detail exactly where he was in the period immediately before and after the Norcroft accident, frequently addressing what he termed 'camp meetings'. These were held, of necessity, on the outskirts of villages, towns and cities, because of opposition locally from both the established church authorities as well as other Methodist factions. An example of the kind of location used is one where, according to Gilbert, "...far more than ten thousand"[25] were present to hear him and others at Wolfstones, near what is now known as Upperthong – to the north west of Holmfirth – on the last Sunday of April 1821. High in the West Riding Pennines, this spot is isolated nowadays and would have been far more so then, with many fewer nearby residents.

The following two Sundays – the 6 and 13 May – saw Gilbert first at Eccleshall and then Burslem, both in Staffordshire, but his journal makes no mention whatsoever of the events of 23 May, by which time he had obviously returned to Yorkshire. However, we are fortunate that the letter he wrote home the following day was published in what appears to be a complete form in a local newspaper over 50 years later.[26]

## JEREMIAH GILBERT'S
## LETTER TO HIS MOTHER ON 24 MAY, 1821

Silkstone, May 24th, 1821.

Dear Mother,

I take up my pen with the greatest sensibility of the presence of God; and by the help and assistance of Almighty Jehovah, I am about to relate to you such things as will cause many tears to roll down your face (if you are yet out of heaven), while you hear the facts, the awful facts related on these sheets of paper.

Yesterday morning, about eleven o'clock, the awful news reached my ears, that eleven persons, men and lads, were coming up out of a coal-pit – when the chain broke, and they immediately fell to the bottom of the pit: five were killed with the fall; one never spoke after; two others died in a few hours after they got home; and another died this morning: so that nine out of the eleven are launched out of time into a boundless eternity, since yesterday morning: and the tenth that I saw last night, if he be living this morning, was to have one thigh set and the other cut off;*[I afterwards saw the doctors set one thigh, and the other was so much

22

mangled that they appeared not to know what to do with it: afterwards they wished to cut it off, but his dear parents were unwilling; yet, after lingering a fortnight in this state, he died and gave up the ghost.] indeed, neither of the two is expected to survive. Yesterday, oh how awful was the sight; for as soon as it was discovered, there were men and women running in almost every direction, both underground and above, to see who had fallen a prey to death's dart; - mothers and wives on the pit-bank, crying, stamping, shrieking, and wringing their hands together; and they who had neither husband nor child in the pit, partook of the general trouble.

There was one man, a father *[This man's loss was very great among the victims; for he had three dear lads; two of them were killed on the place (sic), and the third died next morning: also, his daughter's husband, and husband's brother, all at this time received their death-blow, and are now in eternity], who was at the bottom, and going to come up with those that were killed, but was providentially prevented by a man that begun to talk to him about the prayers of the church. They who first slided (sic) down the rope tell me that the sight was the most awful and affecting they ever saw in the whole of their lives: for some had broken arms, some broken thighs, and others broken legs, feet nearly twisted off, and broken backs; and having their sharp picks and working instruments with them, one had his head nearly off; and there were blood and brains mixed with their victuals. The place where they washed them had the appearance of a slaughter-house.

Now, mother, I will tell you, as near as I can, what I saw with my own eyes, and heard with my own ears.

## Descent into Silence

The first alarm I got was from a woman who came into the house where I sat, and said that two corves *[Corves are what they draw coals up in. I saw these broken corves besmeared with blood and brains.] of men were fallen into the pit, and she was afraid somebody was killed. A few minutes after I looked through the window, and beheld with my eyes a trembling, distracted widow, borne up by two females, one on each side of her. I soon had the great trial of speaking to this widow, and praying with her: her dear partner was a very faithful Class-Leader in our Society, and very much beloved. The night before he got killed he was one of my hearers; and he began the Meeting, and gave out the twentieth hymn in the Ranters' hymn-book; it begins,

> *O God, my heart with love inflame,*
> *That I may in Thy holy name, &c.*

And if you look on in this hymn,

> *Then brothers, sisters, shouting come*
> *My body follow to the tomb;*
> *And as you march the solemn road*
> *Loud shout and sing the praise of God.*

But I suppose that he was not aware that it would be done to him two or three days after; for this was on Tuesday night, and on Friday his body was carried up the streets of Silkstone, and I gave out the very same hymn. After he had given out this hymn on Tuesday night, he prayed very fervently – he prayed for me, and I heard him say, Thy will be done on earth, as it is done in heaven: but I suppose that he did not imagine that the following morning between nine and ten o'clock, it was the will of God that he should drop about thirty-seven yards (with ten others) to the bottom of a coal-pit, never to speak any more.

After having talked and prayed with this distracted widow, I then accompanied her to her own habitation, where I saw two disconsolate sons, one about the age of seventeen and the other about twenty; but to see them cry, wring their hands together, and walk about the house in this distracted state, caused me to shed tears in great abundance. The mother said, "twice before they have brought my husband home nearly killed; but the third time – the third time! they are about to bring him home dead in a cart!" Then the dear lads began to tell their tales of sorrow: for they themselves had only just escaped. A few minutes before they were drawn up, said the son that was about twenty years of age, when I and my brother got into the corve we called out for them to stop, and if they had, my poor father would have got in, and we should all three have escaped the jaws of death: but they did not hear, or did not understand: so they drew along, and we landed safe at the top. Then the others were coming up after us; but when they had nearly reached the top the chains instantly broke, and all fell to the bottom. Then said the young man, I was one that went down: and as I was sliding down the rope, ah! thought I, I must never again see my poor father alive; but when I got to the bottom the first that I saw was my poor father, just alive, but could not speak; and as soon as I moved him he instantly died: then I left him to help the living, well knowing that I could not relieve the dead. The sight

25

was very awful to see; some lying with their skulls open, and blood rolling in torrents; some crying for mercy; and one dear lad singing part of that hymn. Ranters' hymn-book, 31st page, 19th hymn:

> *My soul's full of glory,*
> *Which inspires my tongue,*
> *Could I meet with angels*
> *I'd sing them a song:*
> *I'd sing of my Jesus*
> *And tell of his charms,*
> *And beg them to bear me*
> *To his loving arms.*
> *Sweet spirits attend me*
> *Till Jesus shall come;*
> *Protect and defend me*
> *Till I am call'd home.*

Oh what an awful day will the day of Judgment be: some crying for rocks and mountains to hide and cover them from Him that sitteth upon the throne, and the wrath of the Lamb; others praising God, and rising above the fiery void, and smiling to see a burning world. May we who are yet alive be prepared for the awful day of Judgment.

After having spent an hour or two with this woman and her now fatherless children, I then went along with her to see her lifeless husband; but on our way there she was almost bereft of her senses. We called at George Chisholm's Norcroft, and there I saw another distracted widow borne up by pillows in a chair, where this woman that went with me was put to bed. I and some others then went along to Cawthorne, having arrived there we went up some steps which were besprinkled with blood. We entered the room: most awful sight. On a long table lay five that had been washed, and their bodies bound together as well as they could be, all laid out, wrapped up in clean flannel, with clean caps on and covered with white linen. The first two that I saw were two dear brothers, lying by the side of each other (the third died this morning; three own dear brothers being removed out of time into a boundless eternity, within the space of nineteen hours). The next that I saw, was a pretty looking young lad, apparently about fifteen or sixteen years of age. *[I have been informed since that he was about seventeen years of age.] One of the next two was the Class Leader before mentioned; and I saw then, two of his dear children; a boy between eight and nine years old, and a girl between eleven and twelve. The poor woman, and another of her sons, about twenty years of age, have been in this morning, we prayed with them, and they appeared to be more reconciled to their fate: and the poor woman was constrained to say, that God had done all things well, inasmuch as he had spared her two dear lads, who (as yet) were unprepared to die; she also told me, this morning, that last night she heard some blessed music when she was quite awake; and that she only dozed about fifteen minutes: that during her slumber she saw her husband as plainly as she ever saw him in her life; and he told her about a pound-bill that he had borrowed and paid again; also, that in his breeches pocket that he worked in, there were nineteen pence. She had no knowledge of this pound-bill and she told me of it before she had ever heard of it from any one: and George Chisholm declared that it was exactly as she said; for he was the person that the bill was borrowed of:- further, her husband said that he was quite happy; and she wanted to go with him; but he told her she must not come yet. She saw a white horse and her little daughter running after it; but she cried she would be killed.

Indeed, there have been the most signs in sights and dreams I ever heard talked of, the day and night before it happened.

One saw a white sheet last night near where I sat; he was telling it to Richard Watson's wife, who said, say no more: we shall hear of a sudden death; (and in a few minutes a woman came late into the house and said that Richard Watson had got killed.) besides several other things seen and dreamed of. I, myself, dreamed about being amongst the dead, and seeing coffins; which I had related prior to hearing of the accident, and felt much concerned about my own relations; thinking that either my Mother, my brothers or sisters were dead: and today it is certainly a very solemn sight to see them busy with nine coffins.

On Tuesday, May 22, 1821 a person was working in the same pit, where he heard something scratch in the hole where he was getting coal, like a cricket or a bird in the air; and he thought, the Lord have mercy on us – what is going to befall us; and he felt very uneasy. While he was telling me of it he seemed much cast down. Then he heard it a second time; but it went away towards Richard Watson's hole, and those that were killed; and on the same day a dear lad tells me that he saw four little girls, all dressed in white raiment, that moved very slowly. The lad that saw them is about ten years of age.

About fifteen weeks ago, some men who work in that pit tell me that they heard some clap-doors (through which I have been) clap three times three and then twice: a number equal to the number of men that dropped: nine are dead; two survived a little; one of which is dead since. About half an hour prior to the event, another man said to his wife, what a smell of coffins and the dead.

By the side of Richard Watson, upon the same table, lay another man that was killed: I touched them all and they were then all warm. We left this place, came down the steps, and went into the place where they had washed them, which appeared like a slaughterhouse. But, my Mother, we could scarcely move along without seeing a son weeping and wringing his hands together for the loss of a praying father; a wife weeping, trembling and distracted, then falling into fainting fits for the loss of one of the best of husbands; fathers and mothers weeping over their beloved children, who had black eyes, swelled faces, and nearly every limb in their skin broken, resting in the arms of death; together with their brothers and sisters waiting with anxious desire, with tears in their eyes, and with throbbing breasts, to see them get a little ease or to see them breathe their last.

Dear Mother, this was the sight which I saw, most of the day, wherever I moved. After leaving this awful place, we went to see those who were yet alive, (there being three of them):- the first we went to was a dear lad (whose two brothers lay together dead) with his eyes black, his face swollen, his right shoulder, his arm, thigh, and legs, all broken: indeed, his father said, that he thought nearly every bone in his skin was broken:-

this was the lad that had sung so in the bottom of the pit:-

*My soul's full of glory, &c.*

He anxiously desired us to pray with him. We prayed with him; but he having so much pain, seemed to take little notice:- but this morning, May 24th, 1821, he is gone into a world of spirits.

The next house we went into, there lay an old man, who had not been hurt, struggling and panting for breath, and to all appearances, near his end. *[Two or three days after this, the old man died.] We prayed with him, and then went to see a dear lad, (not hurt,) about seventeen years of age, who was very happy in the Lord. Having prayed with him, *[This dear boy has now gone home to his eternal rest] we left him folded in the arms of Jesus.

The next we went to, was the dear lad that had his thighs so badly mangled:- his father is a Class Leader in our Society and has been a praying man about thirty-four years. We prayed together, and the Lord was very precious to those that waited on Him: but this man seemed to have as much as he could bear: for he had one son that was married, who was gone into eternity a few hours before; and, this lad *[This has also alas, gone into the eternal world, so that ten out of the eleven, are in a world of spirits.] with his mangled thigh, is not expected to continue long. Afterwards, I went to see the son who was married, who died a few hours after being brought out of the pit. Having arrived there, I saw his widow, whose case came the nearest Job's, to my idea of any I had ever seen; for she was sat, mourning, sobbing, crying, sighing, and almost distracted, her husband killed *[These two lads that lay together, were both brothers, and another died this morning after, which was three; a brother killed a while back, her husband killed , and her husband's brother mangled almost to death, and is since dead, six of them belonging to one Family.] also a little child of hers, that cannot run over the floor was crying "Dad, Dad," and she is almost sat down lying again. This woman stands (in) need of God to support her – and He will if she seek him with her whole heart. May the Lord God of Israel support the distressed widows left behind:- also, the fathers and mothers, brothers and sisters, of the dear young lads.

I will now mention a word or two with respect to Richard Watson:- Richard Watson has been a religious man for many years. When I first came into this country (sic), about five months ago, I, through the help of God, preached in his house, from these words: "O, that they were wise, that they understood this, that they would consider their latter end." I began about half-past six o'clock on Sunday evening in January, 1821, and we continued to sing, pray and preach, &c., till about eight o'clock; afterwards we held a Prayer-meeting, when a man began to cry out for mercy, and I was upon my knees with him (and never up,) nearly seven hours; and Richard Watson prayed for him heartily, and fervently, near the whole of the time; at length the distressed man struggled into liberty, when he praised God for the glorious things that He had done for his soul, and is become a most precious man of God, and has been instrumental in the hands of God in the conversion of others.- A woman, also, the same night, found peace with God. – The Lord hath converted souls in this dear man's house. I have seen Richard myself, in very great earnest for the salvation of souls, in his own house; but he is now gone home to glory.

A few weeks after this night of praying, Richard Watson was taken very ill, and to all human appearance likely to die: but God raised him again, but he was, in a short time after, killed in the pit. After his restoration to health, prior to being killed, he began to be more diligently employed in the service of God; and two or three days before the fatal accident, he told George Chisolm, (one of our Preachers,) that he had never been so happy in his life, as he had been since he joined the Ranters. George Chisolm spoke to Richard Watson and several others, in the pit, two or three days before they were killed, and prayed with them. It was a most solemn time for several of them believed that they were unprepared to die:- however, ready or not, in a very short time after, death came and took away six with one blow.

On the 22nd May, 1821, I preached at Silkstone, from 1 Peter, v. 10. "But the God of all Grace, &c." I took occasion to say, that God would give living grace, and dying grace, to every Christian; yet I was not apprehensive that Richard Watson (one of my hearers,) would stand in need of the dying grace of God, the following morning, between nine and ten o'clock. I expected this to be my last time at Silkstone, and I bade farewell to the saints at Silkstone, also to the sinners of the same place.

This was a weeping and melting time: likewise, a rejoicing time. Richard Watson told it afterwards, in a friend's house, that he was never so happy before, during his life, and believed that he wept half an hour without intermission. This was the last discourse he heard in the land of the living. The next morning, in the pit, he was improving (sic) his time by relating to the men and lads, what he could remember of the discourse. He told them that the preaching the night before was about the grace of God; that God would give living grace, and dying grace, to every Christian, and that he would help the Christian in time of need. His widow tells me, this morning, that after the preaching the night before he died, that Richard said, he thought he was never so happy before in his life: never so softened, never so melted down in the whole of his existence. He talked (to his wife) of the things that would be wanted at the Love-feast, the following Sunday, May the 27th, and anticipating that it would be a happy time:- and a happy time, undoubtedly, it would be to him, for there is no doubt that he would be telling his experience among angels, prophets, apostles, martyrs and Christians;- nay, amongst all the assembly of the first-born in heaven, and singing unto him that loved us, and washed us from our sins in his own blood, and hath made us kings and priests unto God and his Father; to him be the glory and dominion for ever and ever. Amen. Rev. 1 - 5,6.

The Wednesday morning on which he died, his widow says that he prayed louder in secret, before going to his work, than she had ever heard him before; she thought that he was reading in some book, but listening more attentively, she found that he was breathing out his soul in mighty prayer at the throne of grace and praying to God to preserve him unto eternal life. I believe that Richard is now wearing a crown of life and that he is treading the golden pathways of heaven for ever and ever.

## Descent into Silence

Last night I went to Norcroft, and they were very busy with the nine coffins:- Richard's was just finished. From Norcroft I went to Cawthorne, where they were just finishing the seventh grave. A cart and coffin were brought for Richard; I helped to put him into the coffin, and then to lift him into the cart; I then rode in the cart with him nearly two miles, and then helped to lift him out again. We took him up the stairs, and then unscrewed the coffin lid, and bore up the disconsolate widow till she looked, for the first time, at her breathless husband; then, with trembling, she drew near, and kissed his cold lips, and afterwards she fell on her knees upon the floor, rose and kissed him again. Afterwards, she thanked the Lord that he looked so much like himself. His son believed that there are not many whole bones in his skin; notwithstanding, he looks a very smiling beautiful corpse.

I am now sitting up all night with the widow, and her two sons, &c.

Nine of the victims are to be buried tomorrow:- there will be a great number to see them put into the earth: it will be a day of much crying, distress, gloom, sorrow, trembling, shrieking and lamentation.

Now, my dear mother, I must write you a line or two concerning myself:- I am pretty well in body, and happy in my soul. Within the last three weeks I have been in Staffordshire, at our Annual-meeting, and am appointed to go into the north, bordering upon Scotland; it is about one hundred and fifty miles from your house. The place is called Hutton Rudby, in Yorkshire. I feel very much concerned about leaving Sheffield and Barnsley Circuits, for many appear very uneasy at my leaving them.

I have often dreamed of you (about you being dead) since I wrote the last letter: I am very anxious to see you. I sent you word that I should come in the course of twelve or fourteen weeks, if all was well. But in your letter you say that the fourteen weeks have proved twenty-two weeks. When these fourteen weeks were terminated, the Circuit could not spare me; but I intend coming to Caunton as soon as possible, and I believe you will be wanting to know the time of my arrival; I will tell you as near as I possibly can. Our Quarter Day will be held the 18$^{th}$ day of June, 1821. I have been thinking that I shall get to Caunton by the 24$^{th}$ of June. Mother, be sure to tell Thomas and his wife to pray much, and get prepared for death; for I am aware that death will soon come, and steal away all our family; we shall soon be in eternity, laid low with the clods of the valley, and numbered with the silent dead. Jesus saith, " be ye also ready for in such an hour as ye think not, the son of man cometh." "Be thou faithful unto death, and I will give thee a crown of life." Mother and sister, pray for me, give my kind love to my brother and sisters, also to every enquiring friend.- I remain, your unworthy, but affectionate Son,

JEREMIAH GILBERT

## 5.

# A Journey Begins

THE PLACE name of Norcroft has, for hundreds of years, covered what were originally two distinct and separate farmsteads working which have been parts of both the Banks Hall and Cannon Hall estates. The farmhouse and two barns of what is known as Upper Norcroft, now comprising eight cottages less than a mile from the centre of Cawthorne village, is nominally distinguished from Lower Norcroft, a still-working farm nearby on Silkstone Lane. It is, perhaps, testimony to an area which has, for most of its history, been a quiet rural backwater between Cawthorne and Silkstone that just a handful of families over the years have been content making a living from its land.

Growing up less than ten miles away near Wakefield, I had been taken to Cannon Hall as a child several times but had no notion of any ancestral connections nearby and had never heard of Norcroft. It wasn't until Julia and I began the interminable journey of genealogy that its significance along the way became apparent. Having been given the impression by my father that our Hinchliffe ancestors came from Wales, I was delighted to discover that my great-grandfather had actually been born in Yorkshire at this place called Norcroft, in 1827. My loud audible expression of delight at uncovering this information on a microfiche machine in the Local History Section of Wakefield's Balne Lane Library drew the attention of John Goodchild, then the District Archivist, in his nearby room. Not only could he advise me of the exact location of Norcroft but he had spent a considerable amount of time researching the coal mining in the area in which my family had apparently been involved. His insights were pivotal in what I never anticipated would become a quite lengthy undertaking.

Looking back to try and understand how the local community in the wider Cawthorne area gelled together – if indeed it did – back in 1812 when young John Hinchliffe was born, means contemplating a very different social structure from what most of us are familiar with today. As a 'baby-boomer' born after the Second World War, I have had the privilege of living in – if not an equal society – one which is a good deal more egalitarian than that experienced by previous generations. But I grew up conscious of the fact that it was not that long ago that the 'squirearchy' ruled the roost in most areas and, especially, our rural villages. My late father, Robert Victor Hinchliffe, was born into a coal mining family at Heath, near Wakefield in early 1914, and throughout much of his childhood and growing up was very aware of the authority of the family which had lived for many years in 'the big house' – Heath Hall. Among some of his possessions which I retain is a "To Whom It May Concern" letter evidencing that their opinions held considerable sway locally, even as recently as the 1930s. Written in respect of my father in the middle of the Great Depression, the perceived First Lady of the village, a relative of the longstanding Smyth family – who he would have known through his regular attendance at St. Peter's Church, Kirkthorpe, near Wakefield – certified that she was sure his continuing, lengthy unemployment "was not his fault." Perhaps even more striking is that the hand-written will of my maternal grandmother, Ethel Hinchliffe, made in 1949 when she was living in Kirkthorpe, bequeathed to one of my relatives "the piece of ground held by me by acknowledgement from the Lady of the Manor."

The Smyth family's wealth stemmed from the woollen industry in Bradford and they had been Heath's leading residents from as far back as 1709. The longstanding interconnections of what might be termed the West Riding 'establishment' are exemplified by the fact that – before he had adopted his middle name – Walter Spencer-Stanhope regarded a member of the Heath Hall family, John Smyth, as one of his greatest friends. They had both been members of the Society of the Dilletanti, formed in 1734 by men who, having been in Italy, "were desirous of encouraging at home a taste for those objects which had contributed so much to their entertainment abroad.[27] The contemporary Whig politician, Horace Walpole's, description of the organisation which bound the two friends together was a little more disparaging, giving the impression of an eighteenth century Bullingdon Club: "The nominal qualification is having been in Italy – the real one being drunk."[28]

In later years, John Smyth and Walter Spencer-Stanhope were, together, to play a major role in facilitating the transportation of coal from the Cawthorne and Silkstone areas to markets much further afield, rapidly enhancing the local mining and the employment opportunities for families like young John Hinchliffe's. Smyth – at the time with significant interests in the Aire and Calder Navigation – chaired the inaugural 1792 public meeting in Barnsley which was to secure the initial investors in the Barnsley Canal project. His friend, Spencer-Stanhope, became a major shareholder from this point, investing some £1,600 into the scheme.[29] The Canal Company were to subsequently be among the various local opponents of the later John George Smyth in 1844, when, as Lord of the Manor of Warmfield-cum-Heath, he unsuccessfully proposed bringing a bill before Parliament for the inclosure of Heath Common.[30] But by then, the Barnsley Canal had contributed to a fundamental transformation of the economies of Cawthorne and Silkstone.

# 6.

# A Puzzling Pedigree

WHILE WE can be confident that the coming of the Barnsley Canal to the Cawthorne area is likely to have played a significant role in John Hinchliffe being born in that parish in 1812, there is not much else about his arrival in the world that year about which we can be certain.

Behind the entry on the opposite page of the burials register for 1821 there is little doubt as to the lineage of Sir Walter. His Horsforth Stanhope ancestors had a lengthy pedigree, and the Spencer connection stretches back way beyond their acquisition of Cannon Hall in the seventeenth century. By contrast, we cannot even be sure who John Hinchliffe's parents were. Putting together a picture of the victims of 1821 is comparable to assembling a jigsaw where, not only are key pieces mislaid, but some that are at hand are completely erroneous. Attempting to make some sense of the family relationships and backgrounds of those killed two centuries on is challenging, not least because some of the information we rely upon for insights into the past is either totally inaccurate or completely missing.

Through genealogical research over many years, I have come across at least twenty-five variant spellings of the Hinchliffe surname, a consequence of the fact that many of the parish register entries of it were recorded at a time when the vast majority of the population were illiterate and the vicar or parish clerk simply wrote down their aural understanding of the names they had been given. It was quite common for the person officiating at church ceremonies and recording the registration details not to be from the local area, so the misunderstanding of local accents in the explanation of both first names and surnames is completely understandable. This happened, in particular, with early ordnance surveys. To the south west of Cawthorne, the medieval settlement of Bilcliffe close to Hartcliffe Tower, near Penistone, was recorded for posterity as Belle Clive by surveyors from southern England clearly unable to understand the information local residents gave to them.[31]

Additionally, in a number of parishes it was common practice to record perhaps a week's entire entries in the registers collectively at the same time so what was entered very much relied upon the cleric's individual memory of the event. An added factor in trying to understand the inconsistencies, errors and gaps in the record offered by the local parish registers concerns how conscientious the local incumbent was. It is not unusual to come across the occasional entry containing quite a sharp subsequent comment about a previous parson's apparent indolence in respect of this important aspect of their role. The Silkstone baptismal registers for April 1814, for example, contain two separate notes regarding missing entries from 1801-02 concerning the two sons of James and Sarah Parkinson: "The reason of this entry not being made in its proper place was owing to the neglect of the then curate, the Rev'd Joseph Wilkinson."

As with others at the time, there may have been some difficulties with the Cawthorne incumbent, Edmund (or Edward) Paley, being able to fully understand the strong West Riding accents of his parishioners as he ministered to his congregation during 1812. Rev. Paley had been born in 1788 in Carlisle, Cumberland, where, according to one of his Cawthorne successors, Charles Pratt, his father Dr. William Paley had been an Archdeacon. Bearing in mind that Sir Walter Spencer-Stanhope sat as MP for Carlisle in the Tory cause for very many years, it is likely that his personal connection with the Paleys led to the appointment especially as the Cannon Hall family were major contributors to the Cawthorne living. Pratt recorded that, in 1813, Paley "… was removed to the Vicarage of Easingwold by the collation of Dr. Vernon, Archbishop of York"[32] but it would be unwise to draw any particular conclusions from this description of his moving on.

Nowhere is the point about the difficulties interpreting local records better illustrated than when trying to establish the exact identity of young John Hinchliffe, one of the two eight-year-olds killed. The surname is quite common in the Cawthorne area at the time, with distinct lineages engaged as butchers, stonemasons, woodmen and colliers. Within this latter group there are two boys of exactly the same name born around the same time in the same locality, both with Norcroft connections. William and Ann Hinchliffe, who were resident at Norcroft at the time of the disaster according to the parish registers, baptised their son John at Silkstone on 18 April 1813 and with William's father being a collier, it is likely that he too would eventually have worked in the local pits. It is documentary evidence from many years on which suggests that this John survived into later life and had married Hannah Heppenstall at Cawthorne during 1840. The couple were recorded in the 1841 census living next door to his parents and four younger siblings at Barnby Furnace, with William still working as a coal miner. John is noted as having the same occupation.

Reports of the inquest into the deaths of twenty-six children in a drift mine between Dodworth Moor End and House Carr collieries in 1838 – what became known as the Huskar or Husker Disaster – refer to the evidence given by a John Hinchliffe. He had been the engine tenter at Moor End at the time a huge deluge caused the tragedy and for a while rendered his "water engine" unusable for either pumping water or drawing colliers out of the pit. It has not been possible to confirm beyond reasonable doubt that this John Hinchliffe was William and Ann's son but he was described in the inquest report as being of "Silkstone Low Mill"[33] which is only a short distance from the family's previous home at Norcroft. He appears the only one of this name involved locally in coal mining at the time and was still living nearby at 14 Barnby Furnace in 1861, by which time the couple had produced some nine children. Hannah is listed as Mary then but as Hannah again by the 1881 census when they are residing at 21 Havelock Street, Barnsley, with John still listed as working as a coal miner. From early on in the nineteenth century, giving girls two names had become an established practice[34] and Mary Hannah is used within the wider Hinchliffe family more than once.

The other John Hinchliffe unfortunately left no similar detailed genealogical trail beyond his baptismal record and later burial entry, immediately opposite that for Walter Spencer-Stanhope in the Cawthorne register of 1821. But he did raise some interesting questions about his antecedents. The baptismal register indicated that he had been born on 30 July 1812 and baptised some weeks later on 6 September. Unlike some of the later baptismal records in both Cawthorne and elsewhere, those around the time of his birth gave no indication of actual parental abode within the parish and unusually in this case detailed no paternal occupation. All we are told about this John is that he was the son of John and Mary Hinchliffe. Frustratingly, a new standard format for entries in Church of England registers was introduced not long after his birth, on 1 January 1813 which was to include more information.

The burial register of 1821 acknowledges just the barest detail of John's age of eight years and an abode, which is noted merely as Norcroft. A John and Mary Hinchliffe are recorded as having lived there in subsequent years but there are no local baptismal records of any other children being born to them. The couple would appear to be the only adults with these names resident in the entire parish during the relevant period but, from the available information, seem to have been too old to have been young John's parents. A Mary Hinchcliff (sic) of Norcroft is registered as being buried at Cawthorne on 11 December 1823, aged 72. The person likely to have been her husband is recorded as John Hinchcliffe (sic) of Norcroft, also being buried there, in his case on 19 August 1833, aged 85. Even allowing for the known inaccuracies in disclosed ages at this time, Mary is likely have been over 60 at the time of a birth in 1812, with her husband probably being around 62.

The parish records evidence the fact that around the time of the 1821 disaster there were four couples named Hinchliffe with given occupations as colliers, all residing at Norcroft. In addition to William and Anne, the parents of the

John who survived into later life, and the older John and Mary, two other Hinchliffe households feature in their pages. Frederick and Mary were living there by 1813, having married at Cawthorne in February of that year. The John Eyre recorded as one of their marriage witnesses was most likely the father of three of the accident victims. Jehoshaphat and Mary were also resident there from around the same time.

Silkstone Parish Church had hosted the marriage of Mary Wilcock to Jehoshaphat Hinchliffe on 2 September 1811. In accordance with the tradition of the time, the bride was wed in her home parish and, while the groom's abode is noted as Cawthorne, he is likely to have been both living and working at Norcroft by then. Their daughter, Jane, who was baptised during March 1814, could have been the first of the significant number of children they were blessed with but, bearing in mind Mary's subsequent pattern of childbearing, it is interesting that, it took her until around March or April of 1813 to initially conceive. With Mary's apparent fertility, this interval of some 18 months since she and Jehoshaphat married leads to the inevitable question of whether the John Hinchliffe was, in fact, their first child and not Jane. As well as the fact that there was a 10-month gap between the date of their marriage and John's birth, there were around 8 months between the time of his arrival and Mary falling pregnant with Jane.

One other possible pointer to the parentage of young John is the frequent practice at the time of naming a couple's first son after his paternal grandfather. Jehoshaphat Hinchliffe was baptised on 5 July 1791, at St Peter's Church, Cumberworth, his parents listed as John, a collier, and Mary, who both seem to have ended their years at Norcroft. Mary was, I believe, John's second wife, his first – Sarah (nee Radley) – having died in 1784. The Cumberworth baptismal register records them having three children between 1776 and 1781, with the first son named John. There is no indication locally that this John did not survive into adulthood making it unlikely that, during his second marriage to Mary, another son would be given the same name. There is the possibility that Jehoshaphat and Frederick were brothers as, in later life, when a widowed Frederick remarried in 1845 after moving to live to the west of the Pennines, the marital record noted his father's name as John.

Whether the Hinchliffes actually lived in Cumberworth at the time of Jehoshaphat's baptism is open to question as parts of that area were actually then within the parish of Silkstone. Where the family came from before then is also unclear but retired college lecturer, Ruth Sheard, has drawn my attention to the possibility of them previously coming from the Calverley area in the west of Leeds. Subsequently, during the seventeenth century, she has noted that James, the son of wealthy Leeds merchant Abraham Hinchliffe[35], had married Ann (nee Purdue or Purdew), the widow of Walter Stanhope of Horsforth, so there may have been some past connection between the Hinchliffes and Stanhopes[36].

Ruth makes the point that, if the Norcroft colliers were actually descended from Abraham Hinchliffe, it is clearly a 'riches to rags' story but she has noted how ordinary families' movements sometimes shadowed those of gentry such as the Spencer-Stanhopes who afforded them employment. Her theories on this lineage might be supported by the fact that, as recently as the late nineteenth century, Walter Spencer-Stanhope's grandson, Walter Thomas William Spencer-Stanhope, retained the title of joint Lord of the Manor of Cawthorne and Silkstone, as well as Cumberworth, Horsforth and Calverley. The possibility that the Hinchliffes could have been 'camp-followers' some years earlier is worthy of further research.

Not surprisingly, Jehoshaphat's name is found to have been abbreviated in later records – to Jesh't, for example, in the 1841 census returns – and it is most unlikely that during his lifetime he would have been addressed in full very often. In terms of understanding the information given in 1812, it might be a long shot but there is a possibility "Josh" could have been mistaken for John. We may well never be able to have cast-iron proof that the victim, John, was the child of Jehoshaphat and Mary, but on the balance of probabilities it seems quite likely to have been the case.

# 7.

# Cawthorne, Constituencies and The Commons

A SIGNIFICANT change occurred in Walter Spencer-Stanhope's life within just a few months of John Hinchliffe's birth, as the Cawthorne squire's long Parliamentary career had finally come to an end. Writing from on board the ship *Berwick* on which he was serving, his son William warmly welcomed the news from his mother, sent in a letter sent during October 1812, that Spencer-Stanhope was finally standing down as a Member of Parliament. His letter to his father, dated a few weeks later, on 2 December, said, "…it was with pleasure I heard you were all well and that you had at last resigned from the House of Commons which I think of late you have found too much for you and that London did not agree with you."[37] Although the constituency element of an MP's role would have been considerably less onerous in the days long before universal suffrage, he would occasionally have had to visit Carlisle and the surrounds as well as spend time at Westminster, when lengthy, horse-drawn coach journeys would have invariably involved overnight stays at wayside inns of varying quality.

He had, over many years, been associated with some very influential figures on the national political stage. Walter Stanhope, as he was first known, was born on 4 February 1749 to Walter Stanhope of Horsforth, near Leeds, and his second wife, Ann Spencer. His mother's brother, John, had left Cannon Hall to Walter junior on his death in 1775 and, in tribute to him, Walter changed his surname by Royal Licence to Spencer-Stanhope.

John Spencer was unmarried and, with his passing, the Spencer line became extinct. His brothers, twins Benjamin and William, had similarly both previously died unmarried and his other four siblings were all female. The last of the Spencer line was descended from the John Spencer who had inherited Cannon Hall after marrying Sarah, the widow of Robert Hartley, the purchaser of the house along with its farm and other properties in the Cawthorne area in 1650.

In the decade prior to Hartley's acquisition of the Hall, the ancestors of Walter Spencer-Stanhope had found themselves on completely opposite sides during the English Civil War. The Stanhopes of Horsforth had been staunch supporters of the Parliamentary cause and in 1643 a warrant was issued against brothers Walter and Richard Stanhope as a consequence of them having taken up arms against the King. The Spencers' arrival in Yorkshire may well have been the direct result of the confiscation of their assets by the Protectorate for having actively supported the Royalists.

After he left Bradford Grammar School, Walter Spencer-Stanhope studied at the University in Oxford and took law at London's Middle Temple. At the age of twenty-five, he began a long Parliamentary career which was to last some thirty-nine years with him representing Carlisle (twice),

# Descent into Silence

Haselmere, Hull and Cockermouth. During his time as an MP, the House of Commons was constituted very differently and male voting qualification depended on having a freehold estate worth forty shillings or more per annum. Burgesses were elected by towns, knights of the shire by counties and the established universities had their own representation. It was the era of so-called 'rotten' or 'pocket' boroughs, with MPs returned from settlements with declining and minimal populations, alongside the buying and selling of seats. In their book *The Common People*, Cole and Postgate remark that, "The composition of the House of Commons in the eighteenth century was of a character so eccentric – to use no more severe a term – that it is surprising that it retained as it did the reputation of being in some degree a representation of the people."[38]

What we would now view as blatant political corruption was then regarded as the norm among the narrow strata of society within which Walter Spencer-Stanhope moved. In the two volumes of *Annals of a Yorkshire House*, his niece, Anna Maria Wilhelmina Stirling, details the practises of the time and how he had sought the help of his cousin, Sir James Lowther, also an MP, to secure a Parliamentary seat. Lowther – 'elevated' to the Peerage as the First Earl of Lonsdale in 1784 – was clearly something of a wheeler-dealer in Parliamentary seats and earned himself a number of uncomplimentary sobriquets including, according to Stirling, "the bad earl". To others he was "the Gloomy Earl", "Wicked Jimmy" or "Jimmy Grasp-all, Earl of Toadstool." Describing Lowther's acquisition of the Surrey constituency of Haslemere from a London attorney, Stirling wrote, "Strange, indeed, was the traffic of politics before the passing of the Reform Bill of 1832, when in a free country a London solicitor bought the elective capacity of a county borough as an investment and sold it to the highest bidder."[39] Spencer-Stanhope succeeded Lowther in representing this seat and it is worth noting that Haslemere was one of the 'rotten boroughs' disenfranchised by the legislation of 1832.

What is known as 'treating' electors as an inducement to support a particular candidate has been outlawed now for very many years but, while it was called into question occasionally during Spencer-Stanhope's time, it seems nevertheless to have been quite common. In 1804, Richard Wharton of Old Park, County Durham, lost his seat for giving a dinner ticket to a voter but others guilty of the same practice remained MPs. Stirling herself remarked on these inconsistencies in relation to the political activities of her uncle Walter. "The peculiarity of the fact, however, cannot fail to be remarked, that it should be held legal for Stanhope to pay the voters who supported him £1354, and to expend £883 on refreshment for them at the public-houses, yet that a single dinner-ticket could be made the subject on which a scrutiny should hinge." She concluded that there appeared to be no limit on the drink which could be purchased to induce voters "…but a single instance of solid refreshment having been given could at once be designated under the heading of bribery and corruption!"[40]

Understanding the real character of Spencer-Stanhope is something of a challenge because, as with his memorial at Cawthorne Church, nearly every account of his life is written in the deferential manner of the commoner to the gentry. And Stirling's two-volumes, while questioning of his polling practises, largely reflected what she regarded as the benevolence of her uncle, generally presenting him – unsurprisingly – in a reasonably positive light.

Spencer-Stanhope's contributions during his time at Westminster very much reflected the concerns one would expect during a period in our history when the country faced the perception of a very serious military threat from revolutionary France, and – especially among the British gentry – ongoing concerns over the possibility of domestic political revolution. His speeches in the Commons reflected both the positives and negatives of his personal experience of leading the six hundred strong Staincross Volunteers during the Napoleonic Wars. The semaphore-style shutter telegraph system, for use in the event of a French invasion especially seems to have exercised his mind. His apparent lack of confidence in the organisation of this countrywide alarm system – and possibly his sense of humour – was apparent in comments he made in the House of Commons in 1804, during a debate on the merits or otherwise of allowing volunteer adjutants and quartermasters half pay. According to Hansard, Mr Spencer-Stanhope, "adverted to the erection of beacons, and instanced one in the West Riding of Yorkshire guarded by four persons, one of who had only one leg, another one had only one arm, the third had lost the roof of his mouth, and the fourth was notoriously drunken, and each of these were paid half a guinea."[41]

It is not clear from the report of the debate which local warning beacon, linked via numerous others to the Kent coast, Spencer-Stanhope had in mind. But he is likely to have had detailed knowledge of the one at Woolley Edge between Cawthorne and Wakefield. In an embarrassing incident during the following year, his troops had rallied in response to it being lit by mistake.[42] According to Nicholas Best's book about the battle of Trafalgar each beacon, "…was supplied with eight wagonloads of fuel and three or four barrels of tar. When the French came, they were to burn wood by night to produce a bright light, damp hay by day to produce thick smoke."[43]

# Cawthorne, Constituencies and The Commons

Portrait of Walter Spencer-Stanhope     *Barnsley MBC*

Spencer-Stanhope's Commons contributions evidenced how very seriously he took his role as head of the Volunteers and how he perceived his authority in this position as emanating from his privileged family circumstances within the local community. During one debate on a conscription proposal in 1806, he expressed concern that, "the men who were to be called out under it were not to be under the command of the gentlemen of landed property, their neighbours, and the persons to whom they naturally looked up to."[44] Nevertheless, in the early years of the nineteenth century, the role of what may be described as a much more overt 'ruling class' was of far more direct relevance to the lives of families who lived at places like Norcroft.

**Descent into Silence**

Although he was writing about his native county of Devon, E. W. Martin's book, *The Shearers and the Shorn*, offers a detailed explanation of the kind of social order widely prevailing in other predominantly rural areas. "From about 1800 and up to about 1918...communities (and the poorer or working classes in them) passed through an era of authority. They were dominated by those who owned the land. This system of domination was expressed through the squire's personality, in his family circle and estate, in institutions and parish government...Inside the boundaries of the country estate (and in country rectories) there was affluence leisure and conviviality. Outside it, small farmers, craftsmen and village labourers eked out a bare living...Everyone accepted the fact that the axis of rural life was the country house and the estate."[45]

At Cawthorne's country house it is evident that Walter Spencer-Stanhope was well aware of the significance of his position as this perceived head of the local community. He had grown up knowing nothing but the rigid stratification Martin described and a letter to his mother, sent while visiting Berne, Switzerland, as a young man characterised in quite forthright language, an outlook which would have been by no means uncommon at the time. Describing the frequent practice of the working classes dancing and making merry at weekends, he wrote, "The girls are at least as full and handsome as those of the lower sort in England and dance very well."[46] He would have been used to the kind of society Malcolm Chase described in the year before his death when, "The most powerful forces were pragmatism and social deference."[47] If there was an axis of rural life within the Cawthorne of the early nineteenth century, at its centre was Walter Spencer-Stanhope.

# 8.

# Something of Shattering Importance

WE HAVE lived, during the last few decades, through the profound revolution of information technology and the internet, experiencing remarkable changes within our lives as a result. The coronavirus pandemic, which began in late 2019, has shaped how we earn our living in ways we never anticipated. But these developments are, perhaps, as nothing compared to the transformation of society which was taking place as young John Hinchliffe was beginning his life. It has been suggested that during our occupation of the planet, the human race has really only taken two major steps forward. "The first was when agriculture was pioneered in the Middle East, about 10,000 years ago…The second was what we call the Industrial Revolution…"[48] and coming into the world during 1812, John arrived in the middle of the latter.

What was his home area two centuries ago now features among contemporary portrayals of Yorkshire's most picturesque villages, standing in marked contrast to the traditional industrial communities located nearby. One such, written before the main impact of the pit closure programme notes, "The lungs of the collieries lie in little pockets of unravaged countryside. Among such is Cawthorne, four miles from Barnsley."[49] But much of the area's countryside some 200 years ago would have looked markedly different, as significant industrialisation had begun to make its mark. I particularly recall a conversation many years back with Michael Clapham, Allan McKay's successor as Member of Parliament for the Silkstone and Cawthorne areas, who pointed out to me that these two parishes were pivotal in the years of transformation of British society during the late eighteenth and early nineteenth centuries. While innovations at the likes of Coalbrookedale, Ironbridge and elsewhere in the Severn valley, often lay claim to founding the Industrial Revolution, his view was that these two West Riding villages had also led the way, with some very significant industrial developments during this same period.

Anyone looking at the local history and industrial activity in Silkstone and Cawthorne at this time is unlikely to contradict his argument and the Silkstone glasshouses, for example, based at what is known as Pot House hamlet, are widely believed to be the birthplace of South Yorkshire glassmaking. Two of the most basic components of industrialisation – ironstone and coal – were found locally. There was an ample supply of water needed to power a blast furnace together with the underwood of local coppices providing its charcoal fuel. The Spencer family of Cannon Hall amassed considerable wealth from their involvement in the local iron industry and, from the early 1700s, their share in the furnace at Barnby not far from Cawthorne.

Barnby had been the longstanding seat of the family of this name since Robert, the son of William de Denby and

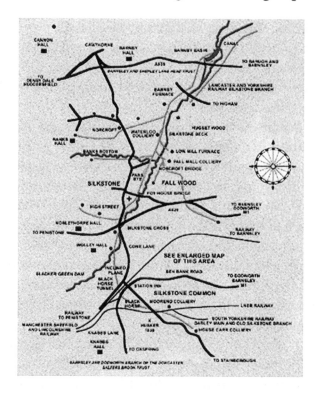

**Sketch map of C19th Cawthorne and Silkstone.** The map was drawn up some years ago by Jim Ritchie, of the Roggins Local History Group. It shows various links to the Silkstone wagonway and its route to the Barnby Basin and Barnsley Canal. The black dots mark just some of the sites of known coal pits

*J. Ritchie*

his wife Sarra inherited eight bovates in the area from his mother in the early fourteenth century. Robert's descendants were among the ruling gentry in this part of Yorkshire, intermarrying with other notable local families when the male line ended during the reign of Charles 1. Barnby eventually came into the hands of the Spencers when, initially, half the estate was sold by Godfrey Copley to John Spencer in 1701 and the other half by Sir John Ramsden to Spencer's son, William, in 1755. A conveyance dated 1673 indicates the Spencers had acquired Cannon Hall from the Hartley family that year.[50]

As the owner of a rich mineral estate, and alongside his political activities, Walter Spencer-Stanhope played a major entrepreneurial role in exploiting these local resources. His family were connected from its very earliest days with the Low Moor Iron Company through John Hardy, an attorney and formerly the Spencers' steward. He had spotted the economic potential of the original Low Moor Estate, near Bradford, and its colliery. After Spencer-Stanhope turned down his proposal of speculating on the venture, Hardy himself entered into partnership with Messrs Dawson and Jarret, purchasing the estate.

It was Hardy who, according to a letter featured by Stirling, advised Spencer-Stanhope in June 1800, of successful coal exploitation on his estate. "I have the satisfaction to inform you that on Thursday last coal at Silkestone (sic), a name I think we ought to preserve as it is in some reputation already, was taken up from the engine pit Eye..."[51] The letter made reference to how well this particular coal burned and the way individual pieces had, "caked themselves with a cinder which was difficult to break."[52] His description of the burning process and obvious delight at accessing a seam of some quality indicates that both he and Spencer-Stanhope had coke in mind, for use by the Low Moor Company. As Yorke's account of the industrial revolution explains, it was "the clean burning 'coke' that was to become the main fuel in the iron and steel industries."[53]

The reference to an 'engine' in coal extraction suggests a location which is much more developed than a mere day hole or adit with a pumping system in place. While an "Engine Pit" was later noted at Lower Norcroft, it seems that Hardy was probably referring to his Low Moor Ironworks partnership working the coal resources on Spencer-Stanhope land. A "pit eye", according to George Redmonds, was a term sometimes used to denote the whole shaft or, alternatively, the pit mouth,[54] but the likelihood is that the reference was to one of the local pits known as "Bye". Correspondence in the Spencer-Stanhope archives dated some years on, in 1834, discusses possible arrangements for the abandonment of a pit of this name and the need to leave a barrier against nearby old workings.[55]

An 1823 plan of the Banks and Silkstone colliery workings actually denotes the existence of two pits of this name. The one Hardy is most likely referring to is adjacent to an "Engine Pit" situated to the south east of Lower Norcroft, with the Wagonway between them and the course of the Silkstone Beck. The other "Bye Pit" is on the opposite side of the Beck, closer to Silkstone.[56]

Pig-iron production had increased four-fold between 1749 and 1788, quadrupling again by the time of the Norcroft disaster. 1779 had seen the landmark building of the first iron bridge over the Severn and the Spencers were in a good position to take full advantage of these rapidly changing times. That year saw an enquiry about the letting of their Barnby Furnace, with a letter from a Fran Dorset of Frodsham suggesting that, "…there is at present a great demand for cannon balls."[57] The conflicts of American independence and wars with France and Spain may have been costing many lives but, as with every other war and national crisis, some – like the Spencer-Stanhopes – would flourish.

Even as late as 1820, they were still seeking the basic raw material of ironstone. In April that year, a letter from

## Descent into Silence

George Hinchliffe of Barnby Furnace[58] told them of the discovery of a bed of it breaking out in Silkstone Fall Wood. Apparently, a servant of the local butcher, Judah Hinchliffe, had found it while, "cutting down some wood in the Bridle Lane".[59] The smelting of iron, using coal, had become established by the middle of the previous century and the mining of it in areas like Cawthorne and Silkstone was fundamental to the profound changes taking place in the world. As Michael Clapham has suggested, these two parishes were key parts of the engine room of this country where, "something of shattering importance to the future welfare of mankind was happening..."[60] A.L. Morton, in *A People's History of England* found it hard to overstate the fuel's role in the remarkable changes. "Without coal there would have been no modern, scientific metallurgy and modern metallurgy is the technical key to large scale industry. Without it the construction of the elaborate and delicate machinery needed by the textile industry would have been as impossible as steam engines strong and exact enough to serve as the source of industrial power."[61]

The coal seams of the area have been known and dug from at least medieval times and the discovery of the clean burning 'coke', following the removal of sulphur, was a significant advance for the iron and steel industries of the West Riding and further afield. The mining of coal locally was at the heart of necessary attempts to improve the local transport infrastructure and, in particular, the development of the canal systems. As coal exploitation significantly expanded in the area, the local domestic markets were increasingly overtaken by those in more distant parts, supplied via the Barnsley Canal from Barnby Basin to the east of Cawthorne, which was connected to the rest of the canal at the beginning of 1802. The Low Moor Company, which was extracting coal at what became known as the settlement of Barnby Furnace, had by then installed a pumping engine taking water back up the five locks at Barugh. From this time, the Cawthorne parish records increasingly evidence occupations connected to the waterway – ship's carpenter, waterman, boat builder – and mention the occasional sailor from distant canal settlements such as Stainforth, on the navigable course to the tidal Trent. In its heyday the Basin would have been a hive of activity and the chutes which loaded coal onto the barges were still visible some years after the canal's closure. The size of the canal terminus and Basin at Barnby and its useage can be imagined with as many as sixty-five barges being seen there when winter weather froze the canal, preventing any movement.

But it is apparent from an examination of the coal exploitation in this area during this period of immense change that its profitability was by no means always guaranteed, as significant capital outlay was needed before the extraction of sizeable quantities. Shortly after the initial availability of canal transportation from Barnby, Joseph Dawson, John Hardy's partner at the Low Moor Company, wrote during 1803 to Walter Spencer-Stanhope in his various capacities as landowner, canal-shareholder and churchwarden, referring to the, "intention of the Town of Cawthorne to assess the lime kilns and colliery", probably at the Basin and Furnace. The assessment most likely concerned liability for the poor rate and he made the point with regard to the colliery that, "so far from its being profitable hitherto that it has been very much the other way."[62] Referring to what was happening where his company was based near Bradford, Dawson wrote, "It is the opinion and practice of towns in this neighbourhood not to assess collieries at all till their incomings exceed their outgoings."[63]

## Descent into Silence

The continuing serious trading difficulties at the colliery were outlined in a further communication from Dawson to Spencer-Stanhope in a letter sent in early 1807, which set out what would at the time have been a staggeringly high loss on the operation. It read, "I am sorry to tell you that without reckoning one farthing for the interest of our larger capital employed in it we have actually lost by the last year's trade not less that £3,659 18s 71/2d. Thus circumstanced it is absolutely out of our power to carry the business on any longer in the way it has been done."[64] Peter Smith's book, *The Aire And Calder Navigation* points out the significance of the unsurprising failure that year of the Barnby Colliery. The construction costs of the Barnsley Canal had, at £95,000, been a massive £23,000 above what had been estimated, and the Barnby shut-down had, "caused an immediate loss of 75% of the coal traffic upon which so much hope and expectation had been built."[65]

It had been the Low Moor Company which was first to act on permissions within the legislation giving the canal's go-ahead, which allowed the construction of tram or wagonways from local collieries to the Basin. Their rail line from the Furnace to the Basin, laid around 1804, was the start of what later became known as the Silkstone Railway or Wagonway. The gradual development of a network of interconnecting rail lines for transporting coal from the various local pits to boat transport moored at Barnby Basin was to have profound importance to the development of the local coalfield in the Cawthorne and Silkstone areas during the early years of the nineteenth century.

The quality of the coal in the Silkstone seam was well known but profiting from its extraction on a large scale had been held back by transport limitations. Although there had been a turnpike road through Silkstone from the 1740s, the generally poor state of the road system in the Cawthorne and Silkstone areas during the early years of the industrial revolution would have seen horse-drawn transportation difficult during many parts of the year. But it wasn't until the 1820s, in the latter years of the turnpike era, that major improvements such as the new Cawthorne to Shepley Lane Head road – the current A635 – began to be seen locally.

The advent of local canal transport and the developing wagonway connections to it were pivotal to that coal extraction. With an eye on increasing its return on the significant investment in the Barnsley Canal, the canal company proposed extending the rail route on past Barnby Furnace to Norcroft and as far as Silkstone as early as 1805, evidencing the fact that a Norcroft Colliery was in operation by then. It seems that, by the temporary closure of the Barnby Furnace pit around the time of Joseph Dawson's 1807 letter, the company had concerns over the reducing tolls for coal transportation and therefore looked to these other sources to not just maintain but increase the boat movement.

**Centre of enterprise:** Banks Hall
C.A. Moxon

# 9.

# Banks and Coal

THE WAGONWAY was of particular advantage to the coal mining activity on the Banks Hall estate which included the settlements of Upper and Lower Norcroft. Banks Hall is located less than a mile-and-a-half to the south of Cannon Hall. Although situated within the Cawthorne parish, the Hall is actually nearer to Silkstone as the crow flies and the estate covered a good deal of what is now open farmland between the two villages.

It is nowadays difficult to imagine that most of this rural landscape would, in the early 1900s, have been at the heart of so much industrial enterprise. However, when walking the area to the west of Silkstone Lane, there are undulations evidencing both this earlier activity and the likely route of a link to the line of the main wagonway to its east. But most of the remaining signs of the extensive mining of the area were obliterated by opencasting during the Second World War when there was an urgent need to increase coal supplies. Geoff Mosley, whose family farmed at Lower Norcroft, says the coal was extracted by dumper trucks and the land reinstated and fenced by German prisoners of war during 1945.[66]

Banks was originally known as Micklethwaite, the likely source of a common northern surname as far back as the thirteenth century when Roger de Milkelthwayt (sic) was noted in the Penistone area circa 1265.[67] A deed held in the Spencer-Stanhope archives from the same period has Richard de Mickelthwayt (sic) as a witness.[68] Its use as a locative name so far back suggests the occupation of Micklethwaite over very many years but, by the late 1600s, it had become "the Bank" or "Bankes alias Micklethwaite". It was for many years the home of the Green family, with Hunter suggesting Ralph Green as the progenitor as far back as 1544-55.[69] Land Tax returns from 1714 evidence the fact that William Green was already working coal on the estate by then.[70]

A list of annual rentals for Banks in 1771 includes a payment of £60 for Banks Colliery which was then being worked by Thomas West[71], whose son, Jonathan, was tenanting both Upper and Lower Norcroft in 1790, according to the Land Tax Returns.[72] Thomas was described as a farmer at his son's baptism in 1751 and, while he is also likely to have farmed, Jonathan was registered as an attorney in apprenticeship returns for 1766, 1769 and 1777.[73] The location of this particular colliery is believed to have been on the right, towards the end of what is now the tree-lined approach road leading from the junction of Woolstocks Lane and Norcroft Lane to Banks Hall, opposite the field path leading in an easterly direction to Lower Norcroft. West, at the time, was occupying Lower Norcroft Farm with Thomas Woofindin the tenant of Upper Norcroft, then itself still a working farm. The Woofindin family followed the Mosleys at the farm which

**The former Upper Norcroft Farm:** As viewed from the south side of Upper Norcroft Cottages                                    *C. Walley*

was in that family's ownership during the seventeenth century. Their surname is recorded in the Cawthorne area as far back as the Poll Tax of 1349.[74] The local parish records contain many generations of their different branches and we know that a John Mosley was at Norcroft from at least as far back as 1611.[75]

A local land survey of 1648 notes Norcroft's two farmsteads, distinguished by "Over" and "Nether", again being worked by a John Mosley.[76] It was probably this same John Mosley who was described as a 'yeoman' when, following his death, a detailed inventory of the Upper Norcroft farm was completed on 4 November 1650. As David Hey has pointed out, until 1858, it had been the Church's responsibility to prove a will and such inventories had been common from the time of Henry VIII. "It was the practice of the church courts to insist that the executors appointed three or four local men to make 'a true and perfect inventory' of the personal estate of the deceased" which were usually attached to either the deceased's will or letters of administration if no will had been made.[77]

The inventory of John Mosley's property gives the clear impression of a quite well-off family, listing all the items contained in the main house and the separate sun parlour, parlour, new chamber and porch chamber, all four of which appear to have been used for sleeping in. The milk-house contents are also listed alongside iron bound wains, ploughs and other evidence of arable farming, together with livestock and significant stocks of stored cereal.[78] Subsequently, the Woofindens had an association there which is noted in several Cawthorne Church memorials stemming from around 1688[79] – when John Woofinden was buried. Forty years later they were still resident there when William Woofinden's will was before a probate court in Doncaster in 1728.[80] The Mosley connection with the locality continued through to current times and they were farming at Lower Norcroft until as recently as April 2007.

The Banks Estate had been advertised for sale during April 1771 and John Spencer of Cannon Hall expressed interest in its purchase. The vendor, William Green, in a letter to Spencer's brother William concerning the possible sale of Longley's Farm – then part of the estate – reflects Benjamin Spencer's outlook of the time, in a letter sent during November of that year. As well as remarking on the serious illness of the Princess of Wales, Green wrote about an earthquake which had occurred in Jamaica on 3 September. "I do not hear of much damage being done, only some negroes killed by the fall of chimneys (sic)."[81]

Although the Spencer family do seem to have purchased Longley's Farm, correspondence in the Spencer-Stanhope archive indicates that the sale price for the estate's entirety exceeded their valuation.[82] The Greens eventually sold Banks to the Fawkes family, then of Farnley near Otley, although it has been wrongly suggested that it was added to the Cannon Hall estate when the owners, "went on the Grand Tour and mysteriously disappeared, swallowed up, it was presumed, in the French Revolution".[83] Anna-Maria Wilhelmina Stirling, who stayed at Banks during the nineteenth century with her two aunts, the unmarried daughters of the first Walter Spencer-Stanhope, wrote extensively of her time there and is credited with this account. Her suggestion that her ancestors may not have been happy about the Greens' occupancy of what may have been deemed part of their local empire, seems nearer the truth.

The Fawkes were, even then, one of Yorkshire most long-standing families and were recorded in the Otley area as far back as the thirteenth century.[84] The first fully published census return in 1841 evidences their continuing prosperity, with them being in a position to employ twenty male and female servants at Farnley Hall. Ten years later there were fifteen tending to them and their guests but the then head of the family, Francis Hawksworth Fawkes, was also employing ten labourers to help farm his 340 acres.

The Fawkes' family clearly sub-let Banks Hall on a regular basis during their ownership from the 1700s. Stirling makes reference to the "laughing parties" held there by Parson Phipps who she describes as "hearty as a buck,"[85] so it seems that the Vicar of Cawthorne was the tenant there during the latter years of the eighteenth century. Rev. Samuel Phipps, who would also appear to have been a regular visitor to Cannon Hall, had become the incumbent of Cawthorne in

1776, with the Spencer-Stanhopes being quite substantial contributors to his living. He had previously been vicar at neighbouring Denby from 1751. One history of Yorkshire examining this period suggests, "The social life of the county was dominated by an alliance between country gentry and the established church,"[86] and these connections are clearly apparent in Cawthorne parish. The Spencer-Stanhopes' land-agent at the time, John Howson, noted that their payment of "a year's dues" to Phipps in 1790 amounted to £11.8s.4d. This amount may have been some form of commutation of local tithes, later finally formalised in law in 1836, but it does appear the traditional contribution of produce still continued. A payment of £2.5s.6d. in October of the previous year, noted as "F. Fawkes, Esq. Tithe Corn Rent," suggests that Banks Hall Farm held Cannon Hall's oblation.[87] Phipps died, aged 85, in 1799 and was buried at Silkstone. Subsequent correspondence with Walter Spencer-Stanhope suggests he was, for his time, quite a wealthy man, with a "residuum" of over £13,000 when his affairs were finalised.[88] Phipps was succeeded at Cawthorne by Paley's predecessor, Rev. John Goodair, who served until his death during 1809.

Francis Fawkes senior, a Whig landowner, had – perhaps unusually, for someone in his social position – been a staunch supporter of the anti-Corn Law movement, opposing restrictions on free trade. He is known to have leased land to the partnership of John Moxon, Dalla (or Dalley) River and Burdett Hawcroft, who were mining coal in the Norcroft area in the latter years of the eighteenth century. Moxon and Hawcroft are listed as regular suppliers of substantial amounts of coal to Cannon Hall at this time.[89] But it would seem that Fawkes himself also at times worked pits there on his own behalf as Howson records a number of payments directly to him for coal bills. These individual bills were by no means insignificant, with the Spencer-Stanhopes paying, for example, three separate amounts of £4.13s., £6.10s. and £5.5s. during just the Autumn of 1789 and a further £4.4s.6d. in January 1790.[90]

It is clear that much more significant extraction of coal on the Banks estate began after Samuel Thorp became the Fawkes' tenant. The Land Tax Returns record him there by 1798,[91] around the time, it has been suggested, that it was the vogue for the merchant/industrial class to have a country seat.[92] The arrangements which took place here are a classic example of what became the increasingly common practice of mining being undertaken by entrepreneurs who were completely separate business entities from the actual landowner. It is arguable as to whether this distancing of the process of coal extraction from the local landlord was a factor in them being seemingly oblivious to its human costs. Fawkes was receiving a significant rental income from Banks and there is nothing to suggest that he, at any point, questioned the manner in which Thorp was earning the money to pay him.

John Goodchild, in his detailed account of the development of the Barnsley coal industry, argued that it was the Thorp family who led its rise and were key figures in the way it was shaped.[93] Prior to his move to Banks, Samuel Thorp had lived at his family's home at Gawber, near Barnsley, and as well as involvement in mining, they had also worked extensively in glass production. His father, William Thorp, came originally from Castleford, a glass-making centre, and from the mid-1730s, was resident at Gawber Hall. He had married Martha Woodcock at Darton Church in 1734 and when Samuel, their fifth child was baptised there in 1749, his father was described in the parish register as "William Thorp, Yeoman." Goodchild suggests that William had

**Portrait of Samuel Thorp:** Painted by his cousin, Paul Tate, and believed to date from around 1780, when he would have been aged just over 30                                                *H. Polehampton*

arrived in the Barnsley area in the 1730s, but it is highly likely that his family had been in the locality from some time earlier. The Castleford parish registers record a Guilielmus Thorp of Cawthorne marrying Edan Pindar there in 1723, and there are two baptisms of boys of the same name noted there in 1695 and 1696. This Christian name – a variant of William, it has been suggested[94] – seems to have had recurrent use by the Thorps, as the parish records at Ledsham, near Castleford, as far back as 1617 note the marriage of Guilielmas Thorp to a Francisca Garforth of "Farborne", which is most likely nearby Fairburn.

It is very difficult to establish with certainty the Thorp male lineage in these old records and particularly to ascertain the exact identity of the Guilelmas Thorp described as "de Houghton", who is buried at Castleford in 1723. Although the Thorp Gawber Hall papers suggest William Thorp was a grocer before moving to the Barnsley area,[95] the subsequent pre-fixing of "Glass" to the Houghton place name raises the possibility that the family were not completely new to glassmaking on their arrival. Interestingly, it seems that the suggestion he was a grocer arose from a misunderstanding of the Latin for 'yeoman' within these papers.[96]

William Thorp's wife, Martha, was the daughter of Thomas Woodcock, who was described as a 'husbandman' and of Gawber Hall at the time of her Darton baptism in 1714, and this may have been the initial Thorp connection specifically with Gawber. The term 'husbandman' ranked Woodcock lower on the social scale than 'yeoman' and it is possible he was working for George Coldwell who is also noted in the Darton records as being resident at the Hall around the same time but described as a 'farmer'.

Hugh Polehampton, a descendant of the Thorps, has pointed out that when Gawber Hall was eventually sold in 1821 it was then actually two houses and had three terraced cottages in its grounds.[97] During the previous century it does appear to have accommodated a number of families and was the case when William Thorp arrived there. His sister, Ann, had married Richard Tate of Kippax and their son Paul married Anne Longley of Raw Green, near Cannon Hall, at Cawthorne in 1736. The couple's two sons, Richard and William, who grew up at the Hall, became well known artists and William was to paint a portrait of Samuel Thorp senior.[98]

The Thorp family were still engaged with the glass business around the time Samuel arrived at Banks as they were supplying bottles then to the Spencer-Stanhopes on a regular basis.[99] While Samuel exploited local coal in the immediate area, his brother, Richard, was to carry on with glass until his death in 1783, reputedly a result of drowning while crossing a river in flood.[100] William Thorp was recorded as far back as 1772 – three years before he died – as a subscriber at a meeting about the establishment of a navigation to Barnby Bridge, near Cawthorne.[101] As the canal was finally connected to Barnby in 1802, Banks coal was taken to it in carts on a summer-only road but Samuel was to take full advantage of the commercial opportunities the wagonway connection would eventually facilitate. Just seven years later he was building a railway from the Banks estate which would connect with it to the south of Barnby Furnace.[102]

# 10.

# Norcroft's Coal Community

FROM AROUND 1800 to the outbreak of World War One, the growth in employment in British coal mining rose from around 50,000 to more than a million.[103] The documented numbers involved in the industry in the early years of the nineteenth century in the Silkstone and Cawthorne parishes, shows it as a minority occupation at the time.

The Militia Lists for the area in 1806 indicate that, of seventy-four males between the ages of eighteen and forty-four in Silkstone, a total of eleven were involved in coal mining. The figure for Cawthorne was thirty-two out of a total of two hundred males within that age range.[104] Obviously, it is important to take account of the fact that these figures relate only to adult males involved in mining activity. We know that during this period considerable numbers of women and girls were engaged in both underground and surface work and that boys were employed in pits from an early age. Also, of necessity, males would have worked

Upper Norcroft cottages                                    *C. Walley*

underground above the age of forty-four and for as long as they were able in an era long before the introduction of pensions.

Before around 1700, coal mining was often a part-time activity combined with agriculture or other occupations such as inn-keeping. But one can see from the contents of parish registers the evidence that coal mining was increasingly common as a specific single occupation from the early year 1900s as larger and deeper mines gradually replaced the day-holes or adits. The activities of entrepreneurs, such as Thorp at Banks, brought labour from further afield, drawn usually by word of mouth. By the 1780s, colliers were being attracted by advertisements in newspapers which would be read aloud in public houses and it was necessary to offer accommodation for these colliers and their families within a reasonable distance of where they would work.

The Land Tax return for 1790 recorded Jonathan West as the Fawkes' tenant of both Upper and Lower Norcroft[105] but Thorp's arrival was to bring significant change, with the old Upper Norcroft farmhouse and its two adjacent barns being converted into as many as eighteen separate dwellings. In his book *Aspects of Life in Old Cawthorne*, D.J. Smith suggests that it was during 1818 that the Thorps, "working the Norcroft and Barnby pits," undertook these alterations[106] but local parish records evidencing habitation would seem to give credence to Charles Pratt's assertion in *A History of Cawthorne* that the conversion took place not long after the start of the nineteenth century[107] and shortly after Samuel Thorp is believed to have taken over the colliery workings on the Banks Hall estate. A 1798 list of Cawthorne householders states Norcroft then to have been occupied by William West, George Anby, George Thornley, Jonathan Charlesworth and Edward Shaw, presumably along with their partners and families[108], but the Land Tax returns also have Samuel Thorp as Fawkes' Norcroft tenant that same year.[109]

The detail in the 1798 list and the subsequent local surveys contained in the Spencer-Stanhope archive[110], evidences the significant population growth in the parish in less than a quarter of a century. The 1798 survey found its total population at the time to have been 999, with 481 males, 518 females and 205 families. Two years later a survey undertaken by Thomas Eyre recorded 1,055 residents and one undertaken by James Wigglesworth in 1811 noted a significant growth in a decade to 1,208.

The list taken by John Livesley, recorded as 1 June, 1821, will have, sadly, included within the population accounted for those victims of the Norcroft disaster towards the end of the previous month, who lived within the Cawthorne parish. His total of 1,518 is a further significant increase and a breakdown of the occupations among the recorded 293 inhabited houses evidences the extent to which industrial activity was by now economically more significant than farming. He records ninety-one families engaged in agriculture whereas 164 families made a living "by working at some trade or other handicraft work." Livesley suggested some fifty-eight families made their livings in other ways.

By 1813, the Cawthorne parish register began to record colliers living at Norcroft but it is likely some of those previously recorded as being of Cawthorne could have been resident there, with both Upper and Lower Norcroft being located in that parish. During the years between 1813 and 1819, twelve families resident at Norcroft had their main paternal occupation listed as collier. In addition to the family of young John Hinchliffe, there are also the Dickinson, Fountain, Gummerson, Healey, Hough, Jagger, Malkin, Pickard, Sadler, Sidebottom and Sidney families recorded. We know the Forden (or Fording / Faulding / Foden) family were also living there some years before the accident and some accounts of it refer to another child victim called Charles Foulding. The source of this information was likely to be the Barnsley Independent newspaper's report of the death of the disaster's sole survivor, Thomas Fox, in its edition of 31 May 1884. But there appears to be no evidence within the local parish records of the existence of this child or a family of that name and it seems likely that Foulding has, at some point, mistakenly been recorded as a variant of the surname Forden.

In trying to understand where the men, women and also the children of these local families were actually employed, there is the challenge of attempting to evaluate the sometimes conflicting accounts of where the coal was being worked at the time. Joseph Prince's 1922 history of Silkstone is "respectfully dedicated" to the parish's miners and

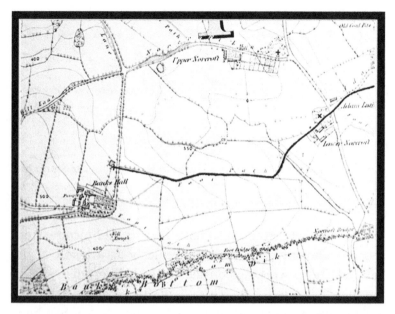

**Map of Banks Estate:** Illustrating course of wagonway from Banks Hall colliery                                                                 *J. Ritchie*

includes significant detail of industrial activity in the district during the eighteenth and nineteenth centuries. From his account, it is apparent that there were two known pits at Norcroft as well as at least two others situated elsewhere on the Banks Hall estate. He distinguishes between the Norcroft and Upper Norcroft pits, Banks Hall and Banks Bottom.[111]

Of course, as well as being the owner of the Barnby Furnace land and a major shareholder in the Barnsley Canal company, Walter Spencer-Stanhope owned a considerable part of the route over which the wagonway eventually ran. From 1810 when the line was fully opened, and in addition to the growing returns on his canal shareholdings, increasing use of the waterway increased the tolls paid to him for barge

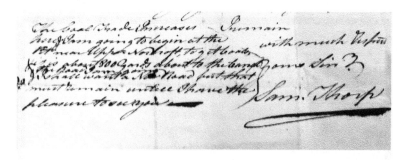

Part of 1814 letter from Samuel Thorp to Walter Spencer-Stanhope.
*Barnsley MBC*

movements. He would also have had further income from the rail movement of coal, particularly as a result of the Samuel Thorp workings on the Banks Hall estate. A list of payments headed "Mr Thorp" in the Spencer-Stanhope archive, for example, indicates that he paid Spencer-Stanhope £20 in 1811 for four years' rent of the railroad.[112]

Correspondence from Thorp to Spencer-Stanhope, dated 16 May 1814 refers to increases in the local coal trade and clearly distinguishes between two Norcroft pits. He indicates that he is "…going to begin at the pit near Upper Norcroft to get coals. It is about 800 yards about (sic) to the canal road."[113] The legislation permitting the Barnsley Canal scheme had enabled lessees such as Thorp or the colliery owners to claim wayleave rights to a maximum of 1,000 yards to their wagon road or canal. In a paper on the Silkstone coal industry written many years later, G.H. Teasdale, whose family had come from County Durham to the area around 1804, refers to "Norcroft Banks…and Banks Bottom."[114] In looking at the use of different names for what may have been parts of the same colliery operation, it does seem clear that the term 'Banks' was used collectively to describe the various pits which were being worked at different times on the estate.

An undated map of the Banks Hall estate, held by the British Coal Authority, and probably drawn up concerning its sale following Francis Fawkes' death in 1818, sheds some light on the probable identity of some of the pits and is of help in trying to establish their possible location. It marks three "old pits" to the south east of Banks Hall, one of which is near to Banks Bottom dike and likely to be what was known as Banks Bottom. Areas surrounding Upper Norcroft and Lower Norcroft are separately marked "Coal got by Mr. S. Thorpe". The Upper Norcroft area includes Botany Bay pit which is located just north of the junction between Norcroft Lane and Silkstone Lane. It is a matter of speculation as to whether this pit was so named because it was first worked around James Cook's arrival in Australia in 1770 although local historian, Jim Ritchie, has suggested that the Botany and Van Dieman's pits may have been so named to remind the local workforce of the very real threat of transportation. The undated map further shows that, at the eastern edge of the Lower Norcroft area, Engine Pit is marked, just north of Lower Norcroft Farm, to the western side of Silkstone Lane.[115] It is not clear if this map is a copy of the one referred to by John Goodchild which relates to workings on the Banks estate on 1 January, 1818[116] but unlikely as that predates Fawkes' death.

A document from some years later, when the Thorp family are ceasing their exploitation of Banks, gives a possible clue to the author of the plan around the time of its acquisition by Walter Spencer-Stanhope. Dated 21 May 1835 and concerned with a financial settlement around the Thorps' withdrawal, it makes reference to the acreage being mined, with that detailed in what is termed "Blenkinsop's survey"[117] being apparently deemed the baseline. It seems that the renowned mining engineer, John Blenkinsop, may have been engaged to survey Banks around the time of the earlier change of ownership. His connection with the Middleton Colliery, near Leeds, is recalled particularly for his invention of the rack railway there in 1811 and the establishment of its steam railway which still runs to this day. Blenkinsop was commissioned by local coal owners around this time to advise on their colliery operations.[118]

The exact location of the Norcroft (as opposed to Upper Norcroft) Colliery has been the subject of some contention. Gary Hawley has suggested that old pits which are marked on an 1855 Ordinance Survey map, just off Adam Lane to the east of Silkstone Lane are, "probably where Norcroft Colliery was located". He notes that, "The site is situated on what would be Thorp's private wagon way" taking coal to Barnby Basin and the Barnsley Canal.[119] Such a location, however, would have been some distance from the areas shown as being worked by Thorp on the undated map, and Brian Elliott has put forward the far more plausible possibility that the pit "may have been located near to Norcroft Farm."[120] Bearing in mind Samuel Thorp's reference to "the pit near Upper Norcroft" in his 1814 letter,[121] it seems most likely that what the undated map notes as Engine Pit, currently marked by a capped off shaft just to the north east of Lower Norcroft Farm west of Silkstone Lane is the site of the main Norcroft Colliery.

From a historical perspective, it is very fortunate that this colliery was the subject of a remarkably detailed illustration, sketched by a noted artist from the period, John Claude Nattes, while it was still in operation. Nattes' biography is somewhat contradictory, with doubts about both the date of his birth and the location and date of his death. The likelihood is that he was born around 1764-65, but where exactly is not entirely clear. The *National Dictionary of Biography* describes him as exhibiting at the Royal Academy

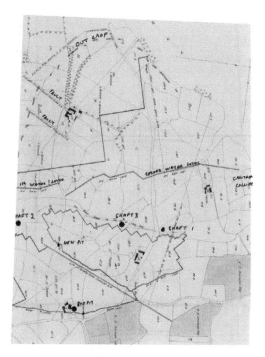

**Blenkinsop survey of Banks Estate:** Prepared following the death of Frances Fawkes during 1818. David Flack has noted on it the locations of several known pit shafts, with 'Shaft 3' likely to have been where the 1821 accident occurred. Cawthorne is to the right (north), with Silkstone to the left (south)                    *D. Flack*

from 1792 to 1804 but implies he may have been a rather controversial figure. It records him as, "One of (the) artists associated in the foundation of the 'Old' Society of Painters in Watercolours. He contributed to their exhibitions up to 1807, in which year he was convicted of having exhibited drawings that were not his own work. Nattes was therefore expelled from the Society."[122]

During the first quarter of the nineteenth century, Nattes had marketed his services as a drawing instructor

## Descent into Silence

**A sketch of Norcroft Colliery:** By John Claud Nattes c.1807

*Barnsley MBC*

based on him having been a pupil of the Irish artist, H. P. Deane. His trade card put forward the case that he, "respectfully acquaints the Nobility and Gentry that he teaches Drawing in the manner of that celebrated Master, on moderate terms..."[123] and the nobility at Cannon Hall were impressed enough to recruit him to give artistic tuition to the Spencer-Stanhope children, when he drew a number of impressions of local scenes including that of the Colliery. Nattes sketchbook, *Views From Nature*, portraying these scenes, is believed to have been completed during August, 1809, although Barry Jackson has suggested there is evidence he may have been giving tuition at Cannon Hall some two years earlier.[124]

According to the *Dictionary of National Biography*, Nattes died in London in 1822 the year following the Norcroft disaster but other records suggest this information is incorrect. The 1839 Index to *Death Duty Registers* actually records his death in Dover, Kent, during that year and noted his residence as St. Germain, France, raising the question as to whether he was travelling between countries at the time. His executor listed in the register was a Joseph Barber of Clapham Rise, Surrey, who was likely to have been a relative through his marriage to Sarah Barber, and possibly his brother-in-law. Sarah is named as Nattes' nominee and beneficiary in a Tontine Annuities scheme, common during his lifetime. The Tontine documentation noted his residence in St Germain but recorded him as "formerly of Welbeck Street, In the Parish of St Marylebone in the County of Middlesex."[125] He was buried in Cowgate Cemetery, Dover, on 14 September 1839 after a service at the local Church of St Mary The Virgin.

In addition to Nattes artistic influence within the Spencer-Stanhope family, it is worthy of note that the son of Cannon Hall stonemason, William Atkinson, also went on to become a watercolour artist of some note. Born in Cawthorne in 1799, Thomas Witlam Atkinson also began as a stonemason but became a noted architect, involved in the design of the rebuilt Barnby Hall and many buildings of significance across the Pennines in Manchester. "Presented at Court to Queen Victoria and praised for his success by Charles Dickens", according to one newspaper article at the bicentenary of his birth,[126] Atkinson produced numerous watercolour sketches and was a regular exhibitor at the Royal Academy in London. *The Hidden Artists of Barnsley* devotes a whole chapter to his remarkable life[127] and a plaque to his memory was unveiled in Cawthorne Church during 2015. Whether Atkinson was influenced by possibly meeting Nattes as a child is a matter of speculation.

From the information that is known about the

## Descent into Silence

Norcroft disaster we can be clear that the pit involved was a deep mine, not a drift, with a shaft up which both colliers and coal were conveyed. As seams had become deeper the task of conveying the extracted coal to the surface was more of a problem. It had previously been possible for the colliers to carry it in baskets on their shoulders up ladders. But exploitation at much lower levels increasingly required mechanisation and the earliest winding apparatus was the hand windlass, similar to that still used on manual locks on inland waterways. As increasing depths and heavier loads necessitated greater power, horses were used to power the windlass, a method sometimes known as the 'cog-and-rung' gin. As Redmonds has pointed out, 'gin' was short for 'engine'.[128]

Jim Ritchie has spent many years studying the archaeology of the route of the Silkstone wagonway and its branches and suggests that the Nattes illustration of Norcroft colliery was probably drawn with the artist standing in what is now the garden of Lower Norcroft Farm, looking to the north towards the direction of Cawthorne village. The detailed image of the pit's surface structures shows the apparent use of both a hand-propelled windlass and a horse gin to facilitate movement of the workforce and materials within the shaft. The horse gin mechanism had been in use since the end of the seventeenth century and involved a horizontal drum working on an upright spindle located some distance from the pit shaft. In the Nattes drawing, the drum which would have been turned by the horses can be seen to the left of the shaft. The ropes winding around the drum would run over pulleys fitted to some headgear over the winding shaft.

The Norcroft sketch evidences the extent of activity at the pit top where work may have been carried out by older

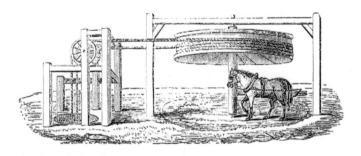

A horse gin of the period          *Children's Employment Commission, 1842*

---

or injured colliers, no longer fit for hewing below ground. Women may have also been employed here and 'pit brow lasses,' as they were known, were working in the coal industry, particularly to the west of the Pennines, until quite recent times. The surface jobs would have been many and varied and some of the tasks undertaken can also be seen in the sketch. Coal is being weighed and carts are moving loads. Chutes, used for loading these carts or possibly wagons for the wagonway, are also illustrated. What cannot be seen are the arrangements there would have been for removing waste material and sorting the coal into different sized pieces, the process which in more modern collieries took place in screens.

Samuel Thorp's exploitation of the Banks estate coal measures took place during a time when mining was moving rapidly from small-scale excavation of drifts, bell-pits or adits to this more sophisticated sinking of shafts to access deeper seams. As the Industrial Revolution progressed, demand for coal rocketed from what was originally needed in the main for limited local domestic consumption to the insatiable requirements of manufacturing production, supplied by rapidly improving means of transport.

**Descent into Silence**

A key challenge, of course, facing those going deeper into the ground was removing the water which so often flooded mine workings. Named after Thomas Newcomen, the first 'Newcomen' steam engine had been used to extract water from a coal mine in Dudley in the West Midlands during 1712, and the designation 'engine pit' at several sites in the Cawthorne and Silkstone area in the early 1900s would seem to suggest the use of such a system. But while 'Engine Pit' is marked on maps at the side of Lower Norcroft Farm at this time, Nattes' sketch appears to indicate that, if a steam pumping engine was in place at Norcroft then, the colliery was still using a horse-gin for shaft winding. It seems strange that the power used for removing water from the pit didn't also automate ascent and descent of the shaft by this time as this had been happening in some other areas before the end of the eighteenth century.

It was not unreasonable for the few individuals aware of and interested in the 1821 Norcroft disaster and knowing that it had been a shaft accident, to conclude that its location had been at the main colliery site and underneath the pit headgear which Nattes had drawn. But the strong likelihood of the accident having taken place instead at the Upper Norcroft location, referred to in the 1814 correspondence between Thorp and Spencer-Stanhope, was confirmed by the unearthing of a mention of a different site in a report in a newspaper in 1884 concerning the death of the only survivor, Thomas Fox. Local mining historian Steve Wyatt has doggedly pursued the full facts around this disaster for many years and, during his research in the local archives discovered the report from the *Barnsley Independent* of 31 May that year, which referred to it having occurred at "the Flatlands Pit, Cawthorne."[129]

Geoff Mosley has, until recent years, farmed at Lower

Norcroft and as an active supporter of the efforts to commemorate the disaster, was able to confirm that although there is minimal documentary evidence of this, the farmland immediately to the west of the Upper Norcroft Cottages and south of Norcroft Lane, has always been locally known as Flatlands. It is open to question whether a document entitled "Butler's observations on Banks Collierys (sic)," contained in the Spencer-Stanhope family archives, was prepared for Walter Spencer-Stanhope when his family were actively considering acquiring the Banks Estate. It has the appearance of an accounts book for Banks, includes the names of tenants and separate individual 'closes' making up the Estate land. Clearly, the existence or otherwise of coal beneath each close was a major consideration for the recipient of Butler's work and ninety-two are listed under Samuel Thorp's name, many with references to "coal got". Alongside one identified close is written "doubtful if coal but clearly not pittable", with several others stating "no coal". There is reference to coal "below Engine Level", most likely a reference to the level at the time being worked at the main Norcroft Colliery, often known as "Engine" at Lower Norcroft.

Of particular interest in relation to identifying the location of the disaster is a description of close 41 as "Lower Fat (sic) Lands" and a reference to a "New Pit Bapit of Botany Bay half got". It is debatable whether what is being described here is half the coal having been extracted from the new 'bye-pit' of the Botany Bay shaft just to the north of the Norcroft Lane/Silkstone Lane junction. And was that 'bye-pit' later to be the disaster shaft Fox referred to as Flatlands? What is clearer from the document is the size of the Lower Flatlands close. It is given as four acres and twenty-two perch, the latter being just over an eighth of an acre, so the land in question would have been a little over the size of four football fields.

## Descent into Silence

The date of the Butler document is not entirely clear but likely to have been 1818, the year in which Francis Fawkes – the estate's then-owner – died at Barnburgh Grange to the west of Doncaster, and shortly before the Spencer-Stanhopes acquired Banks. Importantly, it evidences the clear distinction at that time between Upper and Lower Flatlands on the northern and southern sides of Norcroft Lane.[130]

Walter Spencer-Stanhope had been in Paris when he was alerted to the implications of Fawkes's death in a letter dated 1 February 1818 from the Barnsley lawyer George Keir, who was acting at the time for the Fawkes family but clearly aware of the Cannon Hall interest in Banks. He wrote "I think the Banks estate will be sold, this is at present in confidence to you."[131] Keir outlined the size of the Fawkes landholding in Cawthorne which totalled some 492 acres of land and four acres of woodland.

Led by David Flack, whose family worked the former Hay Royds Colliery at Clayton West, considerable effort has in recent times gone into attempts by the Norcroft Memorial Group to confirm the exact location of the 1821 accident shaft within this sizeable estate and it has been a challenging task, even for someone with a lifetime's mining experience. He has examined detailed underground plans of the former workings, relating them to archival evidence including Butler's report, and contemporary surface photographs of possible past operations. With permission from the family currently cultivating the land in question, during late September 2020 he undertook some surface drilling in the area previously subject to the World War Two outcropping. The drilling failed because the site is covered with fill material which the hand auger drill being used at the time could not penetrate beyond a depth of around two feet. More on-site investigations are planned in the future.

# 11.

# The Millstone of 1812

BURLAND'S ANNALS *of Barnsley* opens its account of 1812 –
the year young John Hinchliffe was born – with a tale
apparently from the naturalist Charles Waterton. It may well
have emanated from the grounds of Walton Hall near
Wakefield, the Waterton family home adjacent to the long
level stretch of the old Barnsley Canal before it dropped
down to join the Calder at Heath.

There was a remarkable description of how the
growth of what was termed a Gilbert tree had raised a
weighty millstone from the ground. The five and a half feet
diameter millstone had been removed from an old property
and discarded within an orchard. Somehow, a bird had
dropped a seed through the 11" diameter centre hole of the
millstone and, "In the year 1812, the seedling of a future
Gilbert tree was seen rising up through the hole."[132] The story
claimed that, "The tree continued to live many years and
gradually elevated the monstrous millstone along with it."[133]

## Descent into Silence

It is difficult to avoid the analogy of young John Hinchliffe also coming into the world with a millstone around his neck because 1812 has, amid significant competition for the title, been deemed "the worst year in British history".[134] The consequence of a twenty-year conflict with neighbours France on trade and prosperity impacted hugely and directly upon the living standards of poor working families such as his. And 1812 was a year of great discord. Spencer Perceval was shot and killed in the lobby of the House of Commons becoming the only British Prime Minister to be assassinated in office. His successor, Lord Liverpool, found himself fighting the United States when they declared war on Britain after the Royal Navy boarded American ships trying to run the blockade against Napoleon. The more significant engagement, the war against his forces, continued on the Iberian Peninsula with the British led by the Duke of Wellington.

But it is clear that conflict wasn't solely international. With the country in the midst of the enormous changes resulting from the Industrial Revolution, bitter battles of class conflict were also being fought on the home front.

The 1799 and 1800 Combination Acts, based on fears of a French-style revolutionary uprising in this country amid the Napoleonic Wars, had toughened up measures already in place preventing the organisation of labour. Early efforts to achieve some sort of statutory minimum wage were thwarted with average real wages stagnating between 1790 and 1814.[135] The implications of Britain's huge population growth added to the adversity facing the labouring poor in areas such as Cawthorne, increasing from just below 11 million in 1801, to well over 16 million thirty years later, with that of Yorkshire's West Riding shooting up by a massive seventy-four per cent. It has been noted that, "...the half-decade before 1820 was the point in England at which the gross reproduction rate reached its highest ever peak."[136]

As Feiling documented, with open strike action deemed illegal, "Left without any weapon except violence, the poor passed through a phase of sharp suffering."[137] Looking through the archives of the Spencer-Stanhopes from this period, the actions having to be taken by some in order to survive are very apparent, with the area's pre-eminent family deeming it necessary to implement quite rigorous measures against poaching by local people on the Cannon Hall estate. Gamekeeper George Shooter emerges as a very significant figure in the accounts of John Howson their land agent, and payments for night patrols to seek out trespassers indicate the extensive steps having to be taken at the time.[138] Others following on in the role during the first quarter of the nineteenth century – George Fisher, Robert Foster, Joseph Green and George Whitfield[139] – are all likely to have more than earned their money, preventing the stealing of game to either feed neighbourhood families or earn income from selling it.

It was a problem clearly being faced not just in Cawthorne. In late 1811, Walter Spencer-Stanhope had received a letter about the issue from Diana Beaumont at nearby Bretton Hall. She attached a press notice which had been issued stating, "Notice is hereby given that man-traps and spring guns are set in the Manors of Bretton, Hoyland, Cawthorne, Cumberworth, Netherton, Haigh, Emley, Barugh and Newall (New Hall)… All poachers or unqualified persons trespassing on the said Manors will be prosecuted to the utmost rigour of the law."[140]

Correspondence from the Barnsley lawyer George Keir to Spencer-Stanhope during 1813 indicated that a former colleague of his in the House of Commons Lord Pollington was keen to join him in the prosecution of "any poacher violations."[141] Pollington – John Savile, Second Earl of Mexborough – had been Tory MP for Lincoln from 1808-1812 and appeared especially exercised over the issue and the activities of one particular alleged miscreant. Keir wrote shortly after Christmas 1813, that he had seen Lord Pollington, "who will join at the expense of prosecuting Whitaker…and desired me to inform you that he would most readily join you in prosecuting any other poacher…"[142] The Spencer-Stanhopes clearly did not hesitate to prosecute, as their later family accounts during August 1821 indicate a payment of £1.12s.0d, "for expenses incurred under the Game Laws in prosecuting (sic) instituted against Goldthorpe and Jackson for poaching."[143] The fate of these two accused is not known but under the night poaching legislation of 1817 – which had significantly strengthened the game laws – a guilty verdict could, by then, have had very serious consequences.

Examining the sanctions for this offence during the early years of the nineteenth century, it is very apparent that landowner-legislators like Walter Spencer-Stanhope had taken the problem extremely seriously at a national level. Initial convictions resulted in hard labour and, from 1800, a repetition earned two years' imprisonment. The use, or threatened use, of weapons to combat arrest would soon become a hanging offence and A.L. Morton describes the growth of poaching at this time as "the class struggle in the countryside".[144] He wrote that, "In 1817 any person not belonging to the class entitled to pursue game who might be found in any park or wood with a gun or any weapon became liable to transportation. In practice, transportation was almost always for life, since no passages were paid home and the transported man rarely returned."[145]

As early as New Year's Day 1812, other signs of serious rural discontent had been in evidence with rick burning some way further south in Nottinghamshire. The Luddite rebellions over the introduction of machines to replace domestic production, which had begun the previous year in the same county, came to a head later that year and the attacks on the mills of the West Riding were all within a day's walk of Norcroft. Smith notes in his history of Cawthorne that, "when there were fears of Luddite riots many workless colliers and ironstone-getters hung around the local markets forcing stallholders to lower the price of butter and preventing them bringing corn into the markets"[146] where, along with other basics like potatoes, its resale price was significantly marked up.

During that spring, at his London house – 28 Grosvenor Square – Walter Spencer-Stanhope received a copy of the notes of a meeting involving the principal inhabitants of the city of Carlisle in his Parliamentary constituency, which had been chaired by the local Mayor. Dated 11 April 1812, it had been, "convened for the purpose of taking into consideration the present high price of grain, and other necessaries, and for devising the most proper mode of relieving the distresses of the necessitous poor."[147] A fortnight later, again in London, he received a letter sent by his agent John Howson from his home in Tivy Dale near Cawthorne, outlining the clear anxieties there were over possible disorder in the immediate vicinity of Cannon Hall. Howson advised Spencer-Stanhope that there had been no "fresh disturbances near us to inform you of" and reassured his master of the local military presence ready to meet with force any threats which might emerge. He wrote of the fact that the Norcroft coal factor, Samuel Thorp, had been visiting his house the day he penned the letter and he had seen "Mr. Wentworth" the previous day. Thorp was most likely referring to having seen Godfrey Wentworth of Woolley Hall, who had been captain of the former Staincross Gentleman and Yeomanry, a man with good knowledge of the efforts being undertaken to contain any challenges to local order.

Howson wrote that Wentworth, "had no fear now - as should the Rioters attempt to come down near us, that the number of soldiers there are placed in so many different situations, with the addition of the Cavalry, would be quite able, not only to keep them off but drive them away..." According to what Wentworth had told Thorp, "...at Barnsley there are Foot and Horse about 250 – also at Penistone and most of the villages near – likewise Sheffield and Huddersfield being not far distant would be more than equal to any number that can come."[148]

It seems fairly clear from Howson's letter that it was ongoing concern over mechanisation which was motivating what he and Thorp saw as mob violence. He advised Spencer-Stanhope that, "Should any attempt be made it must be to plunder the mills for meal and flower (sic)..." What would at that time have been fairly primitive threshing machines were also among the rioters' targets, as they would have been seen as taking agricultural labourers' work. According to Howson, "many (machines) are already taken down and I hope others will do so 'till things are a little more settled." He wished that Thorp would take similar action, adding, "he says they have watched theirs for several nights." It appears Spencer-Stanhope may have had some reservations about an armed presence at Cannon Hall but Howson outlined important steps being taken by others nearby at the time. He understood that not far north of Cawthorne they were, "...protecting Bretton Hall by having a number of men in the House and also have begun in the

Village to Watch and Ward."[149] The instigation of this ancient system of day and night patrols by rotas of local men further underlines the deep unease felt by very many during this period.

Inclement weather over the previous two summers had driven the price of wheaten bread to record levels. Very many folk were at or near starvation level and basic hunger was driving the populous to food riots just over the Pennines in Oldham and Middleton. In 1815, the Corn Law Act had brought back duties blocking cereal imports in order to protect the interests of landed estates, and the consequent artificially high price of staples like bread meant many of the poor in places such as Norcroft faced on going hunger. As Cole and Postgate put it, "Famine was a general as powerful as Ludd: the magistrates denounced alternatively plots to wreck factories and to sell potatoes forcibly at 1$d$. a lb. cheaper."[150]

Walter Spencer-Stanhope, presumably, felt more personally secure at his Grosvenor Square town house, living in a good deal more comfort than the vast majority of his tenants at Cannon Hall. He was able, for example, to provide friends and business associates there with surplus venison from the Cawthorne estate[151] and the finest of wines were being supplied to the family by the noted London merchants of the time, Beldon and Tuck. One letter from them accompanied a delivery on 23 May, 1815 of a dozen bottles of red and white Hermitage at £6.10s, six bottles of Cote Rotu at £3.3s., two bottles of white Burgundy at £1.2s.8d, two bottles of Rio Champagne at £1.2s.8d and two bottles of Barsac at 16s.8d. They had also sent, "two doz Old Bottled Claret which we presume will suffice for the present...as we have plenty of Stout Clarets in the Docks which we shall be bottling..."[152]

# Descent into Silence

Barnsley attorney George Keir was another keeping Walter Spencer-Stanhope abreast of the activities of local agitators. On New Year's Eve 1816, he wrote to him about a public meeting which had been held at May Day Green in the centre of Barnsley on the previous day. The ideas of the radical leader William Cobbett seem to have been central to the aspirations of those in attendance. According to Keir, "Cobbett's observation was blazened forth by the orators... to a large concourse of weavers", although he offered some reassurance that the Yeomanry had been in readiness. "But, after the speeches were over, those attendants and their hypocritical chiefs dispersed and the meeting ended, having first said their intention to petition to Parliament and adjourning to the first Monday after Parliament meets to receive the answer."[153] It was earlier in 1816 that Cobbett had begun the publication of his *Political Register* which campaigned for Parliamentary reform and was increasingly influential in the development of opinion among the working classes.

The very real hardships being experienced by those at the lower end of the social scale during the early years of the nineteenth century are evidenced by where some of the colliers working in the Cawthorne and Silkstone areas during the period originally came from, in their endeavours to find work and feed their families. David Hey has contrasted various studies of the mobility of pit workers later in that century which show that, while in the south west of England, the Welsh borders and the Midlands, considerable distances were travelled, there was rather less mobility of 'immigrant' labour within the West Riding of Yorkshire.[154]

But settlement examinations during earlier years in the Silkstone poor law records[155] show that while some were indeed coming from other parts of Yorkshire to work in the local pits, others arrived from a good deal further afield. Silkstone's William Thompson, aged "about thirty-one" when he was examined in 1816, said he had been born at Seacroft, to the east of Leeds. Some years later, during 1831, seventy-seven-year-old Cawthorne collier Henry Thompson said he originated in West Ardsley, to the ~~west~~ south of Leeds and seems most likely to have been William's father. Another Silkstone collier, William Thomas, believed to be around twenty-eight at his examination in 1817, said he was born in Farndale in what was then the ~~East~~ North? Riding of Yorkshire. Examined in 1822, John Wensley of Silkstone said he was born in Healey, near Masham, in the North Riding, with his father's settlement parish being Reeth in Swaledale. It has not been possible to locate documentary evidence to confirm this, but the Wensleydale and Swaledale connections suggest the likelihood of the Wensley family's previous involvement with extensive lead-mining in those areas. The peaks and troughs of this industry meant many families emigrated at times of hardship, with a few finding mining work in the Barnsley area.[156] Coming from further north than Wensleydale, Silkstone collier Thomas Lewis, aged around twenty-two, said when he was examined in 1816 that he had been born in Newbiggin in Teasdale Forest in the County of Durham. From an apparently much greater distance, William Wiztell, "aged about forty", stated that he had been born in "Ebo, in the County of Kodensburg", in Germany. This claimed place of origin doesn't actually appear to exist but it would not be surprising if those undertaking his settlement examination misunderstood his account, having no knowledge of the country in question and difficulty with his language. "Kodensburg", for example, could possibly have been the Bavarian town of Coburg.

Others in the area were, at the same time, looking to

more distant horizons in seeking a better life. The drastic option of moving not just from the West Riding county but the country was being considered by a number of folk during the later years of John Hinchliffe's short life. Not far from Norcroft, Silkstone's James Harrop, acting on behalf of a number of local men and their families, was actively pursuing the option of emigration to South Africa, alongside other possibilities, by 1819. His occupation, and that of several of the other men he was speaking for at the time, is described as 'farmer' implying possible land ownership and perhaps some wealth. But the term during that time was more often used to describe someone who earned their living in often seasonal farm work and Harrop's occupation is listed in entries in the Silkstone Parish records as 'labourer' which is probably a more accurate reflection of his status.

His letter of 30 August 1819 to Earl Bathurst, the Secretary for War and the Colonies, was prompted by an advertisement in the *Leeds Mercury* of 21 August regarding emigration to what was termed "the new Colony at the Cape of Good Hope". It is apparent from Harrop's heartfelt pleas to Bathurst that his recent reduced circumstances had forced him into bitter experience of the Poor Law. He wrote, "I have been assisted by Town but their hearts are as hard as the nether millstone,"[157] the 'Town' being the township into which the large ecclesiastical parishes were divided for Poor Law purposes. The seasonal nature of the work available locally for himself and others at the time is very apparent from his letter. Harrop added, "Work has been so scarce before the harvest that a man could scarce get employ at all at more than 12/0d per week; and looked on worse than dogs are in general."[158] His appeal for help included the alternative suggestion that the Government might purchase some 500 acres of land which were up for sale at Middop, near

Penistone, on 10 September with the idea of locals being able to obtain small lots for cultivation and a level of self-sufficiency.

A further letter to Bathurst on 27 September makes reference to a meeting held at the Red Lion Inn, Silkstone a week earlier involving James Harrop and eleven others, seven – like him – describing themselves as farmers and three among them miners. It is apparent that, despite their interest in the prospect of the new colony, their circumstances meant that they were unable to meet the costs required to participate in the emigration scheme. On behalf of the group Harrop wrote, "Through the distress of times and badness of trade we are unable to find money for the purport (purpose)."[159] David Hey has noted that such emigration to the colonies – but not to America – was actively being encouraged by government by this time, with some magistrates in southern England regarding it as, "a cure for the problem of a 'surplus population'".[160] The 'new' Poor Law introduced in 1834 saw a reformed administration of the system being more willing to help those who wished to emigrate.

In contrast to the Harrops, matters were very different at the other end of the social scale. The Regency Period had begun in 1810 after the longstanding illness of King George III. The Prince of Wales had brought to the role of Prince Regent substantial baggage of gross over-eating, heavy drinking, gambling and womanising. It is likely he knew little of the lives of his subjects in the coalfields of the West Riding although he did apparently show some interest in Frances, the unmarried daughter of Walter Spencer-Stanhope. It is said that at her coming out in 1817, he kissed her cheek several times repeating the process 'with increased zest and greater noise'.[161] Growing up in her parents' town house in London and the country home of Cannon Hall, Frances would have had the benefit of the well-stocked tables of a wealthy family. The hospitality of the Spencer-Stanhopes was well known and they were proud of Cannon Hall's nickname of 'Roast-beef Hall'.[162] The extensive record of regular payments by them to local butchers Thomas, and later, Judah Hinchliffe[163] suggests an epithet by no means inappropriate.

# 12.

# A Cheerless Childhood

IT IS to be hoped that, for most of his short life, John Hinchliffe would have been unaware of how unjust things were in the world around him. But living within the small community of the former Upper Norcroft farm, in close proximity to a large number of other families, it would surely have been impossible for him to be unaware of the fragility of life. The constantly changing face of the small settlement as families came and went seeking work, would doubtless have been unsettling for a small child, and Upper Norcroft was to be known as "the transit camp" for generations. Current resident Chris Walley understands this term was still being used to describe the cottages even after World War Two.

From a twenty-first century perspective, a family's loss of a child or children is more or less unimaginable in Britain, but 200 years ago infant mortality was a far from uncommon experience and it could be argued that it was rare for a family not to be touched by such desperation, frequently on more than one occasion. In the years before the detailed knowledge and use of various methods of contraception, the average size of families was far larger than is the norm now and the earning potential of children was, for most working-class families, an economic necessity. The deaths of offspring in childbirth or from a range of illnesses and diseases which can nowadays be successfully treated, were not just felt as painful bereavements but also as significant blows to the longer-term financial well-being of the family.

It does not require a comprehensive reading of the burials registers for the Cawthorne and Silkstone parishes to appreciate the experience of local families during this period. Merely looking at what was happening in Norcroft alone paints a clear picture. The Hinchliffe's had the typical experience. Jehoshaphat and Mary's daughter Fanny, born on 10 May 1815 was buried on 20 September of the same year, having died at just eighteen weeks. Their son, James, who was brought into the world on 6 July the following year, lived to be just eight months, being buried on 23 February 1817. Of the other Hinchliffe's resident at the cottages around the same time, Frederick was believed to be Jehoshaphat's brother. Frederick's daughter Ellin, born there on 13 February 1815 passed away aged just fifteen, being buried on 12 May 1830.

Others in the cottages included Thomas Ellam, who was thirteen weeks and three days when buried on 10 July 1814 whilst John and Anne Fountain's daughter, Mary had lived precisely one year and nine weeks when she was laid to rest on 24 June 1815. Richard and Charlotte Sadler's daughter Frances was born at Norcroft on 19 October 1815 and buried on 10 April the following year, having lived just five months. So the list goes on: Anne, the daughter of Edward and Elizabeth Sidney was born there on 24

September, 1816 and buried on 4 February, 1818. David Yeardley was buried on 12 July 1818, having survived just two precious days. Rebecca, the daughter of Henry and Sarah Sidebottom had lived some two years and four months before her burial on 11 July 1819. Little Anne Dyson survived a mere nine weeks in that small community before her burial on 2 September 1819 and, a couple of months later, Tankersley Hill of Norcroft was buried aged five years on 29 November 1819.

All these were mining families, as were the Houghs who seem to have suffered especially during this same period. Parents William and Elizabeth buried their 16-year-old son Sampson on 13 November 1816 and named the child they were then expecting after him when he was born during March the following year. Baby Sampson lived just two weeks before himself being buried on 6 April 1817. The Houghs interred two further children during each of the following two years, Mary, aged ten, on 21 December 1818, and Joseph, also sixteen, on 23 January 1819. As he was growing up, in what limited leisure time he had when he was not working, John Hinchliffe would have played with several of these youngsters before they prematurely died.

It is important to add that any summary of mortality at the Norcroft cottages during the limited lifetime of John will only be partial. The local parish records for Cawthorne and Silkstone during the first year of his life did not include exact locations of residence and some references to the deceased's abode being Cawthorne will probably have related to deaths at Norcroft. It is also quite likely that some of the Norcroft dead will have been taken to more distant parishes for burial, therefore not appearing in local records. While this level of loss of life may have been the norm at that time in many communities, it is still hard to imagine the impact upon young John of living his short life within a tiny

Norcroft Cottages

*C. Walley*

settlement of dwellings which had experienced, at the very least, twenty-three deaths.

In considering the extensive use of child labour at Norcroft and elsewhere at the time of the 1821 disaster, it is essential to appreciate that nineteenth century attitudes to the lives of children such as John Hinchliffe were, often perhaps of necessity, markedly different from those of today. Gardiner and Wenborn make the point that, "The concept of childhood in which children are educated and not expected to work is a relatively modern one, coming to importance in late Victorian Britain."[164] It was during that period in our history that, usually as a consequence of the exposure of their gross abuse in employment, various social reforms gradually began to impact upon the lives of the country's children. The factory system had shifted their labour from the privacy of the family home where, "...it exploited it systematically and often with callous brutality."[165]

Those killed at Norcroft appear to have been leaving the pit around mid-morning at the end of a shift. Under legislation dating as far back as 1802, prompted by the treatment of pauper apprentices, factory owners had faced restrictions on employing some juveniles for longer than twelve-hour shifts, and were forbidden from employing them at all at nights. Not long before the accident, legislation in 1819 had introduced restrictions on the employment of children under nine and also restricted the working hours of those below sixteen but, again, it had focused predominantly on cotton factories.

How young the many boys and girls involved in mining were remained a debateable point and it was a contentious topic when evidence was taken by the Royal Commission which examined children's employment in the aftermath of the deaths of twenty-six youngsters aged between seven and seventeen in the Husker disaster of 4 July 1838, at Moorend, Silkstone Common, only a couple of miles to the south east of Norcroft.

The sub-commissioner taking evidence in the mines and factories of west and south Yorkshire was Jelinger C. Symons and in 1841 he reported being told that children as young as five were being taken into coal pits. With a quarter of a century of experience of working amongst local colliers, Edward Ellis – a Silkstone surgeon – testified that it was common practice in the area for children that young to be working underground.[166] The likes of Ellis and other professionals giving such evidence would have had little to fear from the consequences of their testimonies. But there was concern that the evidence from parents of child workers and the children themselves may have been inaccurate for fear of possible sanctions from their employers. And, as Symons would have understood, for many of the parents who he saw it was an economic necessity to get their children working as soon as they were physically able. The recorded picture may have been a good deal rosier than the actuality.

Whilst its introduction was some years after the Norcroft disaster, the passing of factory legislation in 1833 with a prohibition on the employment of under-nines and a maximum nine-hour day for under-thirteens, may have actually had a detrimental effect on some children in areas like Cawthorne and Silkstone. Because it did not cover industries such as coal mining, the Royal Commission learned that its implementation had actually resulted in their greater use for underground work, particularly in the West Riding of Yorkshire and in Lancashire. Morton suggests, "The fact was that the wages of adult workers were so low that parents were forced to put their children into any occupation that was open for them."[167]

The Royal Commission also commented on the implications of women and younger females being employed underground with particular reference to the dissolute conduct allegedly arising as a result of them being alongside male colliers in a naked or semi-naked state. This issue, it seems, caused considerable disquiet among the Victorian middle classes and apparently troubled the monarch herself. There would probably have been a good deal less anxiety if the domestic circumstances of these mining families at the time had been more widely understood. The cramped and overcrowded cottages of Norcroft, for example, would have offered precious little privacy for washing, bathing, and even procreation, childbirth or dying. Not just different genders but various generations would have been sleeping in the same room.

Although a female employee at a descendent of Thorp's pits is recorded as testifying to the commissioners,[168] it has not been possible to establish any direct evidence of the employment of women and girls at Norcroft at the time of the disaster. John Threlkeld, in his look at the history of mining in the Barnsley area, suggests that the use of women in the local pits had, "started to decline in the late eighteenth century when proprietors found horses were cheaper and stronger in the newly developed thicker seams."[169] The Spencer-Stanhope archives evidence the extensive employment by the Cannon Hall estate of – usually unnamed - women and girls. They are clearly used on seasonal basis for help with harvesting and the family accounts contain many mentions of "sundry women" being paid for such tasks as washing, stone picking and sorting potatoes.

It has not been possible to establish a connection with the Tivy Dale Eyre family which were later to be involved in the 1821 disaster but, shortly before the end of the seventeenth century, Kitty and Elizabeth Eyre each were paid a year's wages of £6.6s.0d for their work as a kitchen maid and dairy maid respectively.[170] It is highly likely that some of the Norcroft females would have sought and undertaken similar roles on the Banks Hall estate during Samuel Thorp's tenancy.

It is difficult to avoid the conclusion that the apparent failure of child colliers to command the serious attention of social reformers during the early nineteenth century stemmed in large part from their relative invisibility. While the factory children, who were increasingly attracting the attention of those concerned with regulating their employment could be seen at times, these young miners often lived in quite isolated settings, like Norcroft, very near to the shaft they disappeared down most days of the week and frequently during the hours of darkness. It is also important to appreciate that there were clear functional distinctions between the likes of Fawkes, and later the Spencer-Stanhopes and Thorp, the colliery operator, as well as the mining families working the pits. This separation created a considerable blurring as to who exactly was responsible for these children working underground in often terrible conditions. Fawkes left all the running of the pits on his land to Thorp. Thorp, possibly via colliery managers, such as John Clarkson Sutcliffe,[171] rewarded the collier in respect of the coal produced, and it was the collier's business as to who from his family – male or female, adult or child - assisted in the process. In other words, underground child labour could be seen as the responsibility of the mining families themselves. And, at a time in our history before the concept of childhood included having an education and not working, their endeavours were essential to these families' prosperity.

Robert A. Roberts' detailed evaluation in the first quarter of the nineteenth century of the mining employment practices of the Clarke family of Noblethorpe Hall in nearby Silkstone,[172] gives a good idea of the arrangements that were likely to have been in place at Thorp's pits on the Banks Estate. It underlines the fact that the collier was an independent operator who would produce a particular amount of coal for the entrepreneur involved, with whom a price would have been agreed. This idea of each individual being a kind of autonomous mining unit is reinforced by the extent to which they often had to fund out of their earnings virtually all the materials needed to undertake their work. Roberts writes that, "Out of the money received the collier would have to pay his hurrier, buy his tools, gunpowder, candles, and sometimes timber."[173]

The specific arrangements varied between the

different mining operators with some directly providing, for example, the collier's tools and levying significant fines if they were lost. At Noblethorpe Colliery, the prices which had to be paid for losses were not by any means insignificant. Riddles, for example, were 3/6d, shovels 2/-, and picks 2/-. A 'peggy' or 'nadge' was a tool with a combined axe/hammer head used for chopping out wooden props. The hammer side was used to re-set the props and this tool would cost 3/- to replace. A hammer was 4/6d, wedges 2/-, with lockers and slippers 9d, and plates at cost price.[174] 'Slipper' was the term used in some coalfields for a form of tub-wheel locker and 'plates' were sheet metal used to manoeuvre tubs, particularly at a shaft side. A list of colliers at Noblethorpe in 1811 shows that each of them had between three and eight picks each and were required to pay for the sharpening of every one of them.[175] The fact that it was later claimed that some of the injuries incurred by the Norcroft victims in 1821 were caused by their tools suggests the practice at Thorp's pits was either for colliers to own them or to surrender them at the surface at the end of a shift.

Children of the ages of the Norcroft victims are likely to have had specific, important roles in the coal getting process underground and clearly worked very long hours. In evidence to the 1842 Childrens' Employment Commission, collier Matthew Lindley gave some idea of the usual arrangements nearly two decades on. "Children are sometimes brought to the pit at the age of six, and are taken out of their beds between 4 and 5 a.m. throughout the year."[176] The youngest and least physically strong would face sitting in the dark for long hours opening and shutting the trap doors helping to control the flow of air in the underground galleries. Redmonds has noted archival evidence of the construction of such doors by blacksmiths, and their operation underground by children, as far back as 1737 in the Nidderdale area.[177] Knowledge of the circumstances of the explosion at nearby Barnby Furnace colliery in 1805, resulting in seven fatalities, would have especially underlined the importance of this role for those at Norcroft old enough to recall it. The leaving open of a trap door overnight had been a key factor in that tragedy and the vital role of 'trappers' within the miners' teams would be fully understood.

Passing through the 'trappers' doors, pushing and pulling the loaded corves (baskets) of coal from the collier at the coal face to the bottom of the shaft was the work of women and older children. This process, in Yorkshire at least, was called to 'hurry,' those involved known as 'hurriers'. In Northumberland, the same role was called a 'putter' and Brian Elliott's Coalminers includes detailed information about children doing this work during the late eighteenth and early nineteenth centuries. Ninety-three-year-old Thomas Batty's testimony recalled, during 1840, his work from the age of six in the pits of Morpeth and he spoke of earning nine pence a day for moving seventy-two corves in a shift of ten to twelve hours. "There were no safety lamps and rails...Boys seldom saw the light in winter."[178] In some pits, there were wagons on rails which would carry the coal underground where bearing barrows had been used in the past. In others, particularly where there were large inclines from the workings, women and children could be found working as 'bearers' carrying coal on their backs on its way to the surface.

There is minimal evidence of any real social interaction between the likes of Fawkes or the Spencer-Stanhopes and when studying contemporaneous accounts of events during the time the Banks coal was being exploited, it is difficult to avoid the impression of markedly polarised and rigidly separated local communities. Burland's account of when, some years earlier, in 1799, the first vessel along the competed Barnsley Canal entered Barnsley Basin typifies attitudes: "Many respectable people were taken on board at the aqueduct..."[179]

Stirling related the tale of her Uncle Walter recording in his journal during 1794, his recollection of a particular incident when he seems to have taken exception to the then legal activity of bull-baiting. He described coming across an excited crowd in Cawthorne, "composed principally of burly colliers and rough loafers."[180] Spencer-Stanhope apparently headed into the throng, driving the man with the bull into the Cannon Hall grounds and refusing entry to his followers. The bull was eventually shot with its owner receiving generous compensation from the squire for his loss. But the juxtaposition of the term "burly colliers" with "rough loafers" perhaps indicates the prevailing attitude towards at least some within the local mining community.

In attempting to understand how the local squire – apparently a supporter of Wilberforce's Commons' efforts on slavery and clearly opposed to obvious animal cruelty – seems, from archive and Hansard records, to have been wholly inactive in respect of child exploitation in his home area, it might be instructive to consider what Stirling's description of the bull-baiting incident suggests. It is common knowledge that during the early years of the 1800s, colliers – as a community – were often viewed with suspicion. Their involvement with such 'sports' alongside a perceived fondness for heavy drinking led to them being regarded, not infrequently, as semi-human barbarians.[181] Even when the Spencer-Stanhopes took over the Banks estate, purchasing it from Walter Fawkes during 1820[182], any hands-on contact with the colliers at local pits would have continued to be the role of the entrepreneurs operating them such as Samuel Thorp or managers like Sutcliffe. The fact that many of the colliers lived very near to their work, in densely populated communities like Norcroft which were distant from the day-to-day functioning of the two nearest villages, may well have reinforced this perception of them being almost a separate breed. The transient nature of such communities will have added to collier families being viewed with considerable misgiving locally.

Frank Machin's detailed history of Yorkshire miners opens with a stark reminder of just how they were viewed around the time of the 1821 disaster: "They have been described, particularly in the first half of the nineteenth century, as reckless, degraded, semi-barbarous, and as living more like savages than civilised beings. They were a people apart and an inferior race."[183] Hugh McLeod's study of them pointed out how some of the colliers were easily susceptible to what might be regarded as extreme political or religious persuasion, "in a world that constantly told them they were rough, uncultured, animal-like…"[184]

## 13.

# The Chiliasm of Despair?

JEREMIAH GILBERT was to remain not far from Cawthorne in the days after the disaster, attending a camp meeting organised by the Sheffield and Barnsley circuits of his church at Mexborough Common, between Barnsley and Doncaster, which was held on Sunday, 3 June. If what happened only a few days before had affected his mood it is not apparent from his record of the day. Noting that, "...the morning was glorious; the sun rose in great splendour..."[185], he appears in good spirits, with the meeting lasting from six in the morning until six in the evening. And if Wolfstones had drawn a good attendance, Mexborough's was even better, with Gilbert recording, "The newspapers reported that there was (sic) twenty thousand people, or upwards, assembled...on this occasion."[186]

An understandable initial reaction to reading Gilbert's earlier dispatch to his mother is probably one of questioning the motives for his apparent close involvement with this tragedy, alongside attempting to extract some facts from the heavy doctrinal content of the communication. All his observations are placed within the strong religious framework which underpinned his outlook on everything that happened in his daily life and an unsympathetic view of the apparent strength of his faith might question his rationality. E.P. Thompson, for example, wrote of "a revival of messianic movements" during the years before campaigning around the 1831 Reform Bill gained the attention of many working-class communities, critically describing the advent of sects as, "…now taking peculiar and perverted forms which perhaps require more attention from the psychiatrist than the historian."[187]

Gilbert's theological roots lay in the Primitive Methodists which had emerged from around 1811 as, perhaps, the most significant challenger to the Wesleyans within Methodist thought. His journals of camp meetings underline a key factor in the difference between these two arms of Methodism, with the Wesleyans fundamentally opposed to an approach they viewed as potentially a threat to public order. At a time when there were still real fears within the British establishment of the repercussions of the revolution in France, there was genuine anxiety over a possible uprising of the dispossessed in Britain. A history of Gatehead Primitive Methodist Chapel – located part-way between Gilbert's Upperthong camp meeting near Holmfirth and Norcroft- suggests that, "In its efforts to prove its loyalty to the establishment and maintain its aura of respectability, the Wesleyan leadership distanced itself from any concept of reform or empowerment of the working classes."[188] John Wesley's death in 1791 lead to a division between those favouring his links with the established Anglican Church and "an increasingly vociferous group which wanted Methodism to go its own separate way."[189] Gilbert was very much in the latter faction.

One account of his grouping within the Barnsley area suggests that, "During the first half of the 19th century Primitive Methodists did work similar to that which is now performed by the Salvation Army. Their aim was first and foremost to preach the gospel to the poor and neglected."[190] While Jeremiah Gilbert was, at this time very much a peripatetic operator, by 1824 the Primitives were later to have their own permanent chapel in John Street, Barnsley known as Wilson's Piece Chapel.[191]

Gilbert's letter might suggest an element of 'shroud chasing' with the description of his functioning around the time of the disaster but Robert Colls has put forward the view that, "At the core of Primitive Methodism during the first half of the nineteenth century was the language of death."[192] Although his examination of the Ranters' approach at this time focused on the coalfield in the north east of England, his book, *The Collier's Rant* offers some possible explanation of the conduct of the likes of Gilbert in the situation he found himself in during May, 1821. "The nearest they could get to knowing (the plan of human existence and Divine Will) was at the deathbed of the believer. The result was a fixation with the experience of death: groups would cluster round a dying man to keep up his morale and satisfy their curiosity."[193]

Just how reliable Gilbert's account of this event was will never be known and some may ask if the passionate religious convictions which so obviously drove his life affected the objectivity with which he reported it to his mother. Should we, for example, take at face value his assertion that one of the dying youngsters at the centre of this tumult was singing hymns at the bottom of the shaft when, as we later learn, his father was of the view that he had broken nearly every bone in his body? Robert Colls' view would probably have been that the lad could indeed have actually sung, even in those circumstances, asserting that – to these believers – "a poor death it was indeed that was not glorified in song."[194] The conviction was that, "it sang out the dead and sang in the reborn."[195]

Gilbert attaches considerable significance to the hearing of something scratching within a hole being worked down the pit on the day before the disaster and noises from clap-doors underground some months previously. The sceptic might suggest that vermin are common in pits where there are remnants from snap tins and that the movements of clap-doors simply evidenced good ventilation. This would have been increasingly important locally after the seven fatalities as a result of the gas explosion at nearby Barnby Furnace colliery in 1805. It would be expected that air flow might result in some door movement but, as Hugh McLeod suggests, for the Ranters, "the most apparently insignificant events of everyday life took on great importance."[196]

What is clear is that during periods when agitation for political improvements in the lives of working people was seen to be delivering very little, religion was turned to. Thompson writes, "whenever hope revived, religious revivalism was set aside, only to reappear with renewed fervour upon the ruins of the political messianism which had been overthrown. In this sense, the great Methodist recruitment between 1790 and 1830 may be seen as the chiliasm of despair."[197] But is EPT correct?

The Norcroft disaster took place during a period when pressure for change was leading to quite radical action in many areas and focussed especially on democratic reforms and the repeal of the 1815 Corn Laws, which were widely felt to be keeping bread prices artificially high. In Malcolm

Chase's detailed study of the events of 1820, he concluded that, "...domestic politics had grown increasingly truculent since the end of the wars against France and Napoleon."[198] What became known as the Peterloo Massacre of 1819 had, he suggested, "a black and enduring significance".[199] The general perception within many less well-off communities was that those responsible for the deaths of eighteen peaceful demonstrators and injuries to almost 700 in Manchester had escaped unpunished while radical leaders, such as Henry Hunt, had been arrested and held. In Barnsley, Burland records, "A great Radical Meeting in the Church Field" being held on Monday 8 November that year. Amongst the banners and flags was a figure of Hunt with an inscription describing him as "The intrepid champion of the people contending for their liberties." Alongside the lists of Chartist demands from the time was the portrayal of "the figure of an infant pointing to the words 'cursed is he that slayeth the innocent'."[200]

It is very evident that the local magistrates in Manchester and elsewhere were deeply alarmed at the huge support demonstrated at these radical meetings, particularly in the Midlands and the North, and their fears were clearly shared at Government level. The so-called 'Six Acts' were rushed through Parliament during Autumn 1819, giving the magistrates hugely increased repressive powers which forced some of those previously expressing legitimate grievances peacefully to consider different tactics. There were tighter restrictions on publishing newspapers and political comment, bans on unauthorised meetings, marching, military training or assembling with banners and flags.

During a debate in the Commons on a bill to prevent drilling and training, James Archibold Stuart Wortley, a Tory MP representing Yorkshire, had drawn specific attention to what had been observed during the evening of 30 November by a colliery proprietor named Faulds while he was riding through the weaving community of Barebones, to the south of Barnsley. Seventy or eighty men were marching around to commands he heard given. "They were next drawn up in a line of three or four deep; some of them were armed with staves nearly eight feet long; he saw them shoulder and ground arms."[201] Wortley claimed to have another letter stating, "that nightly drillings took place, and continued without secrecy, at Monk Bretton and several other villages, as well as at Barnsley."[202] Wortley – later the First Baron Wharncliffe – had previously sat as MP for the 'rotten' borough of Bossiney in Cornwall, from 1797 to 1818, and had served on the Grand Jury at the trial of John Eadon in early 1813 on a charge of administering illegal oaths. The trial was held just after the execution of three Luddites at York and the Burland record had no qualms in also describing Eadon – of Old Engine, Dodworth Road, Barnsley – as a "Luddite."[203]

The so-called 'Cato Street Conspiracy' in London during the following February was a plan to murder the British Cabinet, blocked by the activities of a police spy. In Yorkshire's West Riding during the same month, unionised weavers in Batley had attacked others willing to work for lower prices and caused alarm by rioting in Dewsbury. In his evaluation of 1820, Chase has suggested that around Easter that year, "...the evidence of a co-ordinated campaign of insurgency across several regions...is compelling."[204] The Barnsley area had been a particular centre of concern in terms of agitation with General Byng, the Commander of the Army in Northern England, describing it as, "a very bad place and neighbourhood"[205] so the make-up of the crowd assembled at Grange Moor, between Huddersfield and Wakefield on the night of 11 April, 1820, may have come as little surprise

The subsequently named 'Grange Moor rising' was

made up of men from the Barnsley area who had marched there in an ultimately futile attempt to join an abortive major national uprising. A number of them had assembled at Bank Top, on the Sheffield Road out of the town, with various groups making their way through the night to the meeting point which was equidistant from their home area, Huddersfield and Wakefield. The *Leeds Mercury's* unsympathetic report of 15 April 1820 describes how those involved had begun attempting to gather arms from local inhabitants once they had got some distance from the centre of Barnsley. "At Mr George Hirst's, of Bank Lane, they obtained a gun; and from Mr Richardson, of the Rose and Crown Inn at Darton, after using considerable violence, they collected three guns, leaving a pike and an axe behind them."[206] The group of about 500 arrived around the break of day at the planned rendezvous where, according to the report they were being watched. "Here these poor infatuated dupes had been led to expect they should find 50,000 to 60,000 companions-in-arms, but perceiving that all these flattering representations were mere delusion, they threw away their arms, exclaiming that they had been betrayed."[207]

Cavalry detachments from both the Yeomanry and 4th Dragoon Guards based in Huddersfield seem to have arrived after the marchers had left Grange Moor, but later that day three men were held on suspicion of being involved. On the following day, "the Barnsley troop of Yeomanry were sent to Dodworth...where they apprehended nine men on suspicion of having been amongst the armed men at Grange Moor."[208] Other arrests were to follow including alleged participants from Horbury, and Flockton, near Wakefield and Almondbury, near Huddersfield with, ultimately, a dozen of the alleged participants convicted and transported to Van Diemen's Land (Tasmania).

**Descent into Silence**

The case of one of those sentenced in 1820 to a fourteen-year transportation, 26-year-old Barnsley man John Vallance, who was held in the 'Hulks' at Gosport between Portsmouth and Southampton, is a striking illustration of the genuine predicament many individuals faced at the time in squaring up the need for political action over the sufferings of so many, with a deeply-held Christian faith. Research undertaken by Bob Hinchliffe and published in the *Aspects of Barnsley* series by Brian Elliott, described Vallance as "Barnsley's Chartist Leader". It outlined how his opposition to violence led him to have second thoughts about proceeding to Grange Moor with the others and instead returning home.[209] Unfortunately for him, his presence earlier at a secret meeting place had been noted and he was sent for trial at York. Remarkably, following a local outcry about his case, he was given a free pardon a few months before the Norcroft disaster and allowed to return home.

Like the majority of the Grange Moor contingent, Vallance was a weaver. What seems particularly noticeable, bearing in mind the significant growth of mining in this part of the West Riding at the time, is just how few colliers actually took part.[210] Perhaps that should be no surprise bearing in mind that Burland recorded some 500 looms were employed weaving cloth and check in Barnsley at the time.[211] But the absence of those from the coal trade was, according to Hobsbawn, also the case with other radical and Chartist agitation, "miners...were an isolated body of men, often geographically separated from the rest of the working people and concerned less with politics than with their specialised economic struggles."[212] The colliers at Norcroft would have faced many of these struggles by 1821. Hence, perhaps, their greater susceptibility to the Ranters' message when others in the same locality were planning revolution.

The Chiliasm of Despair?

As with much of this story, the reality will never be known, and it is right to treat what we are told with some caution, particularly where the messenger is someone with Gilbert's doctrinal certitude. The complete, immutable confidence of his beliefs is more than evidenced in the extracts from his journal published three years after the Norcroft disaster. Even just the Preface of this book gives a flavour of the incontrovertibility of his personal faith. In terms of the subsequent text, he states, "There is nothing flowery about it, the Author having stated a few plain, simple, and yet affecting facts; some of which, on being read, have caused the wicked to weep, and the children of Zion to rejoice."[213]

He also clearly has no doubts whatsoever about his personal powers to convert non-believers and the journals are full of the apparently remarkable results of his interventions. On one occasion, while he is in Sheffield visiting a sick woman, he finds himself with another confronting him for making a noise, presumably by loud evangelising. He records, "I met her at the door, got hold of her hand, and spoke to her of death, judgment and a boundless eternity; about the torments of hell, the joys of heaven, and the dying love of the Redeemer. Tears gushed from her eyes, she cried for mercy; and the Lord heard her cry, brought her out of the horrible pit and miry clay, set her feet upon a rock, and made her very happy."[214]

But what is particularly striking to the contemporary reader of both his letter and journals is the absence of specific references to any concern whatsoever about the appropriateness – indeed morality – of the extensive employment of children in work such as mining coal. While the picture one gains of the local Established Church at the time is of it being little less than an adjunct of the local

123

squirearchy, might at least some comment on the injustices of what had happened have been expected from someone so clearly seen as a serious threat by institutionalised authority in 1821? It is also interesting that Gilbert makes no reference to any possible culpability in connection with an episode which has resulted in the appalling suffering he describes. There is no mention of the possible responsibilities of those such as Samuel Thorp or his manager operating the pit and their obligations towards all those directly affected. In his wanderings around the homes of those deeply distressed by this episode, followed by his involvement in at least one of the subsequent funerals, there is no apparent contact with Banks Hall or the Spencer-Stanhopes, by then the owners of the estate on which the pit was being worked.

We learn nothing from him concerning the final journeys of Thomas Townend within Cawthorne, the Eyre boys from Tivy Dale and the two eight-year-olds, John Hinchliffe and Charles Forden, from near their place of death at Norcroft. It is not known whether there was a collective service at All Saints for all these victims. Other than the venue, the only identifiable element in common with the funeral of Walter Spencer-Stanhope just over a month previously was the fact that it was conducted by the same person, the Rev. John Penketh Buce. In a community as small as Cawthorne, it is likely that he would, at least, have had some acquaintance with the families of the victims, albeit not as close as with the squire. Buce was the son of a Liverpool merchant, baptised in 1780 at Our Lady and St. Nicholas, the Anglican parish church of the city, located close to the River Mersey near Pier Head. He and his wife Elizabeth had lived at the Cawthorne Parsonage since at least 1814 when their son, William Urban, was born and named after his paternal grandfather. Four daughters were subsequently born to the couple but, in accordance with everything else in the saddest of years locally, the last – Dorothy – survived just two hours before she was interred at Cawthorne on 18 November 1821. Less than six months on, and not even a year from him conducting the Norcroft disaster funerals, Buce himself was dead, being buried in Cawthorne churchyard at the age of forty-two.

While Gilbert's correspondence is strong on theological content, it does give some outline of what happened on that May day two centuries ago and in the immediate aftermath of the terrible event. We are given a detailed idea of the numbers of men and boys involved, clues as to who some of them were and a clear indication of the nature of what was a shaft accident at the end of a shift. Less clear from his account is the exact location of the shaft involved and we are reliant upon the Thomas Fox obituary of 1884 for some indication of this. While the *Barnsley Independent* report of 31 May 1884 was notionally about the subject of Fox's recent death, aged seventy-nine, it was substantially a rehash of Gilbert's letter on the disaster. Describing his connection with it as "the principal event in his life" it went on to detail the circumstances of the accident. "Eleven persons, including Mr Fox…were being drawn out of the pit which was 40 yards deep, and when they got within sight of the landing board, the chain attached to the corve broke and the whole were precipitated to the bottom."[215] This report, appearing over sixty years after the event, claims the Norcroft shaft to have been some sixty feet shallower than the *Leeds Intelligencer* account of 1821. A later feature in the *Barnsley Independent* concerning the Fountain family suggested that a number of colliers had ascended the shaft immediately before those losing their lives, as we learned from the Gilbert account. It said, of 13-year-old George Fountain that, "He was one of the miners who came up the draw before the catastrophe which caused the death of ten men."[216]

One subsequent description of the event noted that, "an ascending platform carrying men and coal lost its hoist near the mouth of the pit and eleven men and boys (no women and girls) were hurled to the bottom."[217] This account appeared in the local press well over fifty years after the accident happened and its reference to the transportation of coal as well as colliers on a platform, rather than the corve described by Gilbert, perhaps needs to be treated with some caution.

We do not know from the minimal records of the accident the practical arrangements at each of Thorp's pits for raising and lowering both colliers and coal, but we know from Gilbert's recollection of the event that two separate corves carrying the workers were involved. These baskets were still in widespread use at the time of the accident. The Nattes sketch of the main Norcroft colliery site illustrates a more complex operation than applied at Flatlands but shows two pullies at the top of the shaft indicating the likelihood that the use of two corves was normal there at the time.

David Flack, who has a lifetime's experience of mining, has taken a particular interest in the Norcroft accident. He states that, "The common method in all but shallow shafts was to have two ropes on the winding drum wound such that, as the one corve was raised, the other was lowered. So that, for the same number of times the horses(s) went round to fully raise or lower the corves, the capacity was doubled to that of a single rope and the work of the horse(s) reduced a bit by the weight of the empty corve offsetting that of the full one." He continued "To raise two corves side by side would require twice as much horse-power and the rope to be twice as strong and heavy – a significant factor, as when the corve was starting to be raised the total load would be weight of coal + weight of corve + weight of rope."

In terms of the specifics of what happened, his view

An artist's
impression of the
ascending corve
*H. Malkin*

was that, "With two corves and ropes in use in the accident, the corve and men falling down the shaft would collide in some way with the other corve which would be near the bottom and so the result would be that there would be two corves in the condition that Gilbert described. It is likely that there would be men waiting for the descending 'cage' to ride out but, as the corve would not quite have reached the bottom, it is unlikely, but not impossible, that they could be involved in the accident." Gilbert's letter refers to those who had "slided" (sic) down the rope after the accident. David Flack explains that, "With two ropes in use, the rope which was connected to the corve in the shaft bottom would allow the men to climb down it to investigate the results of the accident."[218]

Whether it was chains rather than ropes which had

actually hauled the corves is also not clear. The *Leeds Intelligencer* report of 28 May 1821 talks of a "brig" giving way and specifically of a "chain" breaking. Quite what the "brig" was is not certain either. The term has traditionally described a bridge and possibly the platform on which the corves were landed. But the term could have been used in respect of the winding drum primarily bearing the weight of both corves which, according to Gilbert, would appear to have been hauled. If the drum mechanism had given way, it can be assumed that both corves would plunge to the bottom rather than the higher one just dropping on to the lower and there would have been no second rope for the rescuers to descend.

Machin's history of the Yorkshire miners suggests that at the time of the accident, most collieries in the county would have been using hempen ropes for shaft haulage purposes but notes that at some pits chains were in fact being used by then.[219] The proximity of potential supply of such chains – with furnaces, like Barnby being close by – makes it quite possible that the *Intelligencer* account was an accurate one of the winding practices during the years before wire ropes became the norm. In another examination of coal mining history in South Yorkshire and North Derbyshire, Ken Wain writes of the Norcroft winding chain breaking and the severing of the winding rope. "In the absence of any contrary evidence," he suggests, "one can only assume that negligence in the form of lack of, or no, maintenance was to blame for this needless loss of life."[220]

The Gilbert letter advised his mother in grisly detail of the nature of the injuries incurred by those killed in the shaft plunge and the consequence of one of the corves plunging up to sixty yards to the bottom would have been significantly worsened by the likelihood that sharp tools were being brought up out of the pit at the end of the shift.

Accepting that, without the availability of detailed inquest evidence understanding the mechanical causes of the Norcroft accident will be speculation, it is also worth reflecting on the potential instability of raising and lowering human cargoes within the relatively light corves, which were traditionally made from plaited hazel wands. Fiona Lake and Rosemary Preece in their study of women and children in Yorkshire coalmines during this period, make the fundamental point that, "Getting into and out of the pit was no less dangerous than the rest of the working day."[221] Even if a sturdier cage system had been used at the time at the main Norcroft Colliery, it wasn't until 1835 that guide rails or rods were being fitted within shafts to steady the ascending or descending platforms. Before what became known as the 'cage tub and guide rod system',[222] it is highly likely that, with the use of a horse-drawn pulley system, the moving corves would have been unstable and a possible additional causal factor in the tragedy. Machin notes, for example, that more than thirty years on from Norcroft, a ten-year-old boy was killed at Brick Lane Colliery, Bradford, in 1854, when a corve had swung violently.[223]

The Flatlands operation would probably have been a relatively minor enterprise compared even to the main colliery adjacent to Lower Norcroft Farm. The Nattes sketch evidences the use there of both a hand-cranked windlass and the more powerful horse gin for coal and 'man-riding'. Norcroft Colliery subsequently encompassed the use of a steam engine which is likely to have been used for the key function of pumping out water from underground workings. There is no evidence of any form of engine house at Flatlands so it is most likely that a horse-driven cog and rung gin would have powered the movement of colliers and coal.

# 14.

# The Accident's Aftermath

WHAT IS not apparent from the limited information we have, is the detail of any legal formalities of the time in view of the extensive fatalities. With subsequent pit tragedies in the area, we do know that it was the norm for inquests to be held, usually in a local ale house, with the deceased often on view within forty-eight hours of the deaths, but it has proved impossible to find any record of one being held after the Norcroft tragedy. Nevertheless, the Thomas Fox obituary definitely refers to one saying, "Some survived but a few hours, nine being dead when the coroner held his inquest, one more dying after making ten killed."[224] Until 1826 it was actually a legal requirement for the coroner and jurors to view dead bodies, with most inquests being held within the parish where the deceased had lived.[225]

Gilbert describes, after having spent time in Silkstone with the grieving Watson family immediately after the disaster, going with Richard Watson's widow Mary to

Cawthorne to view his body, visiting Norcroft on the way where it seems she was "put to bed." He speaks of seeing there, "another distracted widow borne up by pillows in a chair" so John Handforth's may also have made her way near to the scene of the tragedy, from her home in Silkstone. His reference to "George Chisholm's Norcroft" implies he knew this person and later in the letter it becomes clear that Chisholm was one of the Ranters' preachers. The fact that, according to Gilbert, Chisholm, "spoke to Richard Watson and several others, in the pit, two or three days before they were killed, and prayed with them", confirms he was working underground at Norcroft. He is likely to have been living in the colliers' cottages but it is curious that no other record of his time in the locality seems to exist. His surname is very unusual for the area, with the only Chisholm family anywhere near being recorded twenty years later, in the first census to be published, living in Thompson Hill, Ecclesfield to the north of Sheffield. There may be a connection to George Chisholm as Hugh, the head of the family, is listed as a coal miner, but the paucity of information about his time in Cawthorne raises the question of whether his prime purpose during a short stay at Norcroft was also one of evangelising in the local community. — not on PM plan, 11/1821

The Gilbert account indicates that, initially at least, the bodies of some of the deceased had been taken to Cawthorne village, although it is unclear as to exactly where. He relates that, "...having arrived there we went up some steps which were besprinkled with blood" and describes entering a room where five of the deceased lay on a long table. If this was the room of a public house where an inquest was to be held then it is likely to have been located in one of the two known to exist in the village centre at the time. Edward Baines's *Yorkshire Directory*[226] published the year after the disaster refers to the Golden Cross, run by Sarah Bell, and the still-licensed Spencers Arms where Dorothy Wilcocks was the landlady. Both these establishments had separate outside upstairs chambers and it has been suggested that either the Harness Room at the Golden Cross or the Band Room at the Spencers may have been the temporary mortuaries. The Spencers' Band Room was the inn's former coach house and the more likely location. Baines also lists John Bashforth's Jolly Sailor inn at Barnby Basin as operating at the time but it is highly unlikely the dead colliers would have been taken that distance from the pit.

It is evident that the bodies of the boys and men had been initially taken to a lower room of the Cawthorne building – possibly a basement or cellar area – where they were washed before, in some cases it seems, having body parts bound together to make the corpses more presentable for viewing by relatives. It is not surprising that this place was said by Gilbert to have "had the appearance of a slaughter-house."

The correspondence enables some idea to be gained as to who was on the table in the upstairs room as he described seeing two of the three Eyre brothers, sixteen-year-old Thomas Blackburn and Richard Watson, whose wife he had left at Norcroft. He described another man laying at the side of Watson who would have been John Handforth. The letter suggests Gilbert had then gone to the Eyre house in Tivy Dale as it described the terrible physical injuries apparent on the body of the one surviving brother he saw there, who was also dead by the following morning.

He also describes next visiting a house where, unrelated to the disaster, an old man is "struggling and panting for breath", clearly near his end. Gilbert appears close to the Eyre home and was likely to have still been in

Tivy-dale. The person concerned was most probably John Howson, who had lived there and was buried, aged seventy-five on 3 June 1821. Burland noted that he had been, "…for many years the confidential and universally respected agent to the recently deceased Walter Spencer-Stanhope"[227] and the Estate records indicate that he had served the family from as far back as 1775 until his death.[228]

"The dear lad that had his thighs so badly mangled" was the next person seen and Gilbert's comment, that his father – "a Class Leader in our Society" – had already lost his married son in the tragedy, indicates that this would have been thirteen-year-old John Townend who had been taken to his home in Cawthorne. The body of John's brother William was then viewed at his home in the village, with Gilbert describing the terrible grief faced by his wife Charlotte, with her multiple losses that day. Her sixteen-month-old son, also called William, was seen crying for his father.

Gilbert writes of being at Norcroft again on the night of the disaster where he observed the completion of the coffins for the nine victims already dead. At Cawthorne churchyard he described seeing the completion of the final grave of the seven being buried there before helping to place Richard Watson in his coffin and travelling with him to his home in Silkstone, where he was taken upstairs for the overnight vigil he spent with his widow and sons. Either Gilbert was mistaken concerning the number of Cawthorne graves being dug or John Townend's subsequent death had been anticipated on the evening of tragedy, which seems unlikely. Townend actually survived for another two weeks with his injuries and was buried at Cawthorne on Friday 8 June. The location of his grave and those of the others interred at Cawthorne is uncertain and it was the position of the Barnby disaster memorial, to the north east of the Church,

Rear of memorial to Norcroft victims     *D. Hinchliffe*

which led to the memorial to the Norcroft victims being located in the same area of the churchyard during 2019. That memorial notes that three of the victims lie elsewhere. Richard Watson's burial took place at Silkstone on the same day as that of most of the other victims and Jeremiah Gilbert's account would seem to suggest he had some role in the funeral service. Thomas Blackburn was buried on 25 May at Darton with John Handforth's funeral being held at Rothwell.

Gilbert's account makes very clear the appalling impact of the accident on the Eyre family of Tivy Dale and the horrifying experience of John Eyre, at the bottom of the Norcroft shaft when his three sons, Charles, aged sixteen, Robert, twelve, and Benjamin, ten, were fatally injured along with his son-in-law, Thomas Townend, aged twenty-three and Thomas's thirteen-year-old brother, John. It is genuinely impossible to imagine his feelings when confronted not just by the ghastly sight of a mass of horrendously injured human bodies but also the recognition that so many of them were his loved ones. The *Barnsley Independent* report of the event which appeared many years later records that "One other brother, William Eyre, who was not working, went down into the pit to assist."[229] He would have been around twenty-two at the time and we do not know if he or John Eyre had to break the news of this tragedy to his mother Mary and it is particularly hard to comprehend how anyone could have passed on the terrible tidings to his sister Charlotte. Expecting their second child in less than two months' time, she had lost her husband – the father of their toddler son – her three younger half-brothers and her young brother-in-law.

John Eyre had been baptised during 1773 at Kippax between Castleford and Leeds. He had married his first wife, Rosannah Boys, at Holy Trinity Church in Rothwell between Leeds and Wakefield, in 1795 and – <u>unusually</u> for a working man at that time – had actually signed his own name after his wedding. Their first child had been baptised at Rothwell in October of the following year and naming her Charlotte may have been prompted by the birth of the daughter of the future King George IV in January 1796. Charlotte Eyre's brothers, John and William, had been born during 1798 and 1799. It was not unusual for women around this time to die of complications during childbirth and this may well have been

x mony could just sign their name

a factor in Charlotte and the boys losing their mother during 1802. She was buried at Rothwell on 14 April that year. The parish register also records the baptism of Thomas Eyre on the very same day. John is recorded as the father but, unlike most of the other entries, no mother's name is mentioned. Caring for four children under seven as well as earning a living will not have been easy at this time for John Eyre and it is no surprise to find that he remarried in October of the following year at Cawthorne Church to twenty-one-year-old Mary Atkinson, who came from the village. His move to the area coincided with significant mining opportunities arising locally as a result of the fact that coal barges could sail from Barnby Basin along the full length of the Barnsley Canal from early 1802.

John and his new wife would appear to have had little difficulty in terms of fertility and, from the birth of son Charles during the summer of 1804, consistently had another child almost every two years until the birth of their final child in 1824, by which time he had fathered fourteen children. Celebration of the newborn was very much accompanied by grieving for those who had passed, occasionally, as with Thomas Eyre's arrival at one and the same time.

Prior to John and Mary Eyre suffering the devastating loss of their sons Charles, Benjamin and Robert on that fateful day in May 1821, two more of their boys had also died. James, born in 1812, was buried at Cawthorne during 1817, whilst Thomas's burial took place at Cawthorne on 11 October 1810 when he would have been eight-years-old. The cause of his death in unknown but it is significant that Jeremiah Gilbert's letter, in describing being with a "widow" who is clearly Charlotte Townend, the sister of the Eyre boys, says she also had, "...a brother killed a while back..." This could, of course, have been the first James who had died just over four years before aged four. But it was more likely to have been Thomas who, being eight at the time of his death and from a mining family, may also have perished through his work. Gilbert's description of the situation implies that this was the case.

Charlotte Townend had married her husband, Thomas, at Cawthorne Church during 1819 and their first child, William was born the following year. Thomas Townend had been baptised at Flockton between Huddersfield and Wakefield during 1798, but an 'Examination To Settlement' of his older brother by the Silkstone Overseers of the Poor during 1816[230] suggests that the Townend family originated in Notton, near Wakefield, where, it would seem, they had been been reliant upon the Parish during his childhood. ·

The Silkstone document certified that when William "was about 8 years of age he was bound by Parish Indenture to Joseph Green of Notton for the term of 21 years, that when he had served Green about 3 months he was regularly transferred by the consent of two magistrates to John Fountain of Flockton…, Collier, and duly served with him the remainder of his term of apprenticeship."[231]

While the Poor Law Acts passed between 1597-1601 had established the township or parish administrative framework for poor relief, subsequent legislation – particularly the 1662 Act of Settlement – had set out the criteria whereby a poor person was accepted as lawfully settled in a parish and entitled to poor relief, if unable to maintain themselves. Such apprenticeship arrangements were a means by which a new settlement could be obtained in an area other than where an individual had been born.

William's apprenticeship most likely saw him working underground, initially as a trapper, from the age of just eight. One history of the industrial revolution in

Yorkshire describes such pauper apprentices as being "little more than slaves"[232] and William Townend's period of indenture continued with him working in the Cawthorne area with John Fountain for the five years before the Settlement Examination.

The complexity of the operation of the Poor Law at this time is particularly apparent from the attempts by the Silkstone Overseers to establish which parish was responsible for Townend, who had married Rebecca Hoyland at Silkstone Church during 1814 and fathered two children with her by the time of the Examination. He had been born in the Flockton-with-Thornhill parish, had been indentured to Green in Notton for just three weeks and then Fountain in Flockton and Cawthorne, but lived and worked in Silkstone where his wife came from. It appears that he had spent less than a month of his life in Notton but, because of his father's origins there, that parish was deemed his legal 'settlement'.

It has not been possible to locate any similar documentation relating to Charlotte Townend's husband Thomas, but his arrival in Cawthorne could well have been by a similar route to that of his older brother. He had also been baptised in Flockton during 1798 as was the other Norcroft victim, his brother John, who was baptised there in early 1808. It was probably the connection of the Townends to John Fountain which resulted in them moving to the Cawthorne/Silkstone area. John Fountain married Ann Green at Flockton in 1796 and the Cawthorne baptismal records record children being born to them – with Cawthorne the abode – in 1814 and in 1818 when living at Norcroft. Fountain is described as a collier in both entries.

The limited records concerning the operation of the Poor Law locally during this time gives the impression of an increasingly complex system which caused the responsible

Overseers a considerable amount of work during their time undertaking the role. The Churchwardens' Accounts for Cawthorne[233] indicate that they had provided "parish houses" for the poor from at least 1689 when they were bought from Sir Thomas Wentworth of Woolley. The Accounts mention their repair during 1765, the "rents of poor houses" five years later, and payments made by the churchwarden, John Kaye, to a mason for repairing "the town's houses" in 1833 just before major changes affecting the treatment of the poor the following year. The 'towns' or townships were subdivisions of ecclesiastical parishes such as Cawthorne. As well as the provision of these houses, it is evident from the Accounts for this period that occasional payments were also made towards the rents paid by paupers, including some from Cawthorne who were residing within other parishes.

By the early years of the nineteenth century, Cawthorne's Overseers were making extensive use of Emley workhouse for the accommodation of paupers from the area who were not being maintained by the so-called 'outdoor relief', which could include top-ups to the earnings of those deemed deserving. The workhouse, located on Out Lane to the west of the village, operated from 1803 until 1835. One bill for the first quarter's use of this workhouse amounted to £9.16s.7d. and the transportation there of one inmate – Ann Hemingway – cost the parish some 3s. Legislation from 1781-82 had required that, "No persons except the indigent were to be sent to the workhouse" and the workhouse accommodating them should be no more than ten miles from their own parish.[234] Statutory measures from the same time required local magistrates to occasionally inspect such workhouses and report on their findings.

The procedures concerning the establishment of

which parish was actually responsible for individual paupers involved the Overseers in extensive travel, usually with the persons concerned, for examinations by magistrates often some distance away and to assize hearings. During the latter half of the previous century, the work of one of them Thomas West of Lower Norcroft Farm, involved him in the expenditure of £1.16.0d for his attendance in connection with a settlement hearing concerning another Hemingway – this time William – at Pontefract Assizes. David Hey has suggested that settlement disputes such as this would make up a considerable proportion of the cases heard at these quarterly court sessions. "Both sides in a dispute employed learned counsel to argue their case. Parishes thought it was worth their while to do so, for losing a case might have meant that they were saddled with maintaining a poor family for ever."[235]

The record of John Stead's period as Overseer at the turn of the century includes many mentions of journeys to Woolley to get people examined regarding their settlement by another of the Wentworth family, who was a magistrate. One such case required payments to former church warden and local butcher Judah Hinchliffe for the use of his cart.

Stead's accounts outline the details of various outgoings at the time under the poor law with "bastard pay" to mothers for maintaining an unsupported illegitimate child averaging 1s.3d. per week. "Bastard pay received" lists identify the various fathers also paying an average of 1s.3d. each week towards the maintenance of children where paternity had been established. Payment of "occasional relief" is detailed, along with help for the cost of funerals, the provision of "coals", and clothing. It was around this time that the increasingly prominent John Livesley featured as "Inspector of the Worsted Manufactory for the Poor" in

Cawthorne, indicating that – for a short period at least – the clothing provided under the local poor law may have been manufactured by some of the paupers themselves, with any surplus from sales going towards the poor rate. Around the time Samuel Thorp had his turn as Overseer, during the early years of his coal exploitation of the Banks Estate in 1802, Livesley handed over £20.4s.11d which was the final balance for the profits from worsted spinning when it was discontinued.

The Manufactory had another role in preparing able-bodied local paupers for employment elsewhere, as did the indenture system which is mentioned in the Overseers' outgoings. The accounts of John Johnson's period as churchwarden around 1834, for example, shows the Parish was taking advantage of industrial expansion not far from Cawthorne, with the expenditure of 6s. on "Journies (sic) to Barnsley with Parish apprentices."[236]

Richard Watson had been one of Jeremiah Gilbert's main local contacts, referred to in the letter to his mother as "a very faithful Class-Leader in our Society" who had been at one of his meetings the day before. Gilbert's account of visiting the Watson family home in Silkstone includes the indication from his wife Mary of his involvement in previous accidents where, "twice before they have brought my husband home nearly killed…" and it is evident that Richard Watson's two sons had been working with him at the time of the Norcroft tragedy. It was normal practice for colliers to work in family groups.

In describing his contact with the Watsons following the accident, Gilbert refers to one of these sons being "about twenty years of age" and this would most likely have been Thomas. He had been baptised at Barnsley St. Mary's Church where his father had married Mary Pickering during 1798. It seems that the family had moved to Silkstone by 1812 where Thomas's brother, Richard, was baptised during December of that year.

Gilbert has given a detailed explanation of young Watson's experience of getting into a corve with his brother at the bottom of the shaft and calling out for it to be held until his father had joined them, "but they did not hear, or could not understand." The consequence was that, while his sons were raised safely, Richard Watson was ascending in a following corve when the link broke. While other colliers who were underground would have been first to the casualties, Thomas Watson seems to have been one of the first to descend a rope from the surface and see the carnage. As Gilbert records, his father instantly died when Thomas moved him.

John Handforth's burial took place on 25 May, the same day as most of the other victims, after his body was taken to Rothwell from where he had originated. At his baptism there, during 1776, John's surname was recorded as Handfirth and several other variants of its spelling are evident in the Rothwell parish records, evidencing the presence of the family there from at least the early years of the eighteenth century. He had married Frances Nother in 1798 and it is most likely he had followed another member of his family to Cawthorne as a Peter Handforth, described as a collier, features in the local baptismal records after he and his wife, Sarah had a daughter, Amelia, in 1806. The marriage of Peter Handforth and Sarah Ely is recorded in the Rothwell records two years earlier.

Sixteen-year-old Thomas Blackburn was the only one of the Norcroft victims to have his final resting place as Darton, to the north east of Cawthorne – nowadays divided from nearby Kexborough by the M1 motorway. From Darton church, Churchfield Lane leads through Kexborough where it joins Cawthorne Lane, with the walk to Cawthorne village centre being some fifteen minutes. Why his family determined his burial should be at Darton rather than Barnsley St. Mary's where he was baptised in 1806, or Silkstone where they were living at the time of his death is unclear. The family's roots appear to have been in Barnsley, although Thomas's father (also Thomas) was working as a carpenter at Fallhead, just to the eastern side of Silkstone beck, in 1819, when daughter Julia was born. Thomas, senior, his wife, Elizabeth and the family were still living in Silkstone when son Joseph was born in late 1820, most likely at the same location which was not far from Norcroft.

Charles Forden's background has been particularly difficult to establish as a direct consequence of the numerous variants of his surname, but he may well have been the youngest victim. While the other eight-year-old, John Hinchliffe was born on 30 July 1812 and baptised just over a month later on 6 September, the baptism of a Charles Falden took place In Alfreton, Derbyshire on 4 October, 1812. Alfreton is a long way from Norcroft but there are some important clues suggesting this boy is the one who was killed in 1821. The baptismal records have his mother as Elizabeth and there was an Elizabeth Fording living at Norcroft around the time of the disaster. A transcription of the father's name in the Alfreton register queries it as being Felghem and an earlier baptismal record for a previous child – also named Charles – in 1810 has the surname as Faulden and the parents as Faeldem and Elizabeth. This Charles would appear to have died at a very young age with his brother, born two years after him, being given the same first name.

Alfreton was a major coal mining centre, and it is probable that the boys' father was working as a collier there at the time of both their births. But, along with the surviving Charles, he and Elizabeth had moved from Derbyshire to the West Riding of Yorkshire by 1813. A Foljambe Falding was remanded to the West Riding House of Correction – what became Wakefield Prison – that year for being in breach of the terms of a Bastardy Order.[237] Legislation dating from as far back as 1576 had enabled local justices to imprison those responsible for an illegitimate child, and Foljambe Falding must have been named by a child's mother as being the father. A later Act in 1733 had required women in such circumstances to reveal the father's identity in order that the local Overseers of the Poor could ensure he paid for the maintenance of the child and it didn't become the sole responsibility of the parish. The legislation made provision for the father to be arrested and held in prison until he was able to come to an accommodation with the parish in relation to his financial responsibilities.

Illegitimacy was a fact of life among colliery workers during the early years of the nineteenth century and it has already been noted that evidence to the Childrens' Employment Commission had highlighted the possible consequences of the underground mixing of naked and semi-naked colliers of both sexes. One male witness to the Commission appeared to point to the culpability of the female colliers in respect of the illegitimacy rates, which troubled the local Overseers. In his testimony John Cawthra, a collier at Messrs. Wilson's pit in Barnsley said, "I do not think it is a good system to bring girls down the pit; they get bold and it tends to make the girls have bastards."[238]

A perusal of the parish baptismal registers around the time of the Norcroft disaster leaves little doubt as to the identity of these illegitimate children. In what is widely regarded as a classic study of parochial administration, *The*

*Parish Chest*, W. E. Tate wrote that, "...illegitimate children are invariably so described in the registers, whether from moral indignation at their parents' offence, or from concern as to the effect their births might have upon the poor rate."[239] He added that, "In the records of their very christenings these unfortunate children were treated with more obloquy than even the most bigoted high churchman used with reference to the children of dissenters."[240] Stories of the pitiless treatment of mothers of such children by the Poor Law authorities underline the lengths gone to in efforts to establish paternity and financial responsibility. It was not unusual for the assistance of a local midwife to be withheld from a mother during a painful labour until she had disclosed the name of the child's father. His identity enabled them to determine which township would be deemed liable for its maintenance.

A hearing at Wakefield Quarter Sessions on 13 October 1813 made an order to the effect that Falding "...be immediately discharged out of the House of Correction... until he settles with the Overseers of the Poor."[241] The likelihood is that he would have been returned there if he had not met his responsibilities towards the maintenance of the child in question. The Cawthorne parish registers subsequently record in 1826 the re-marriage of the widowed Foljambe Faulding of Norcroft to Hannah Moseley. Their children John, Sarah and Harriot were born between 1828 and 1833, by which time the registers recorded a Fuljambe Foden as still working as a collier at Norcroft. His Christian name had reverted to Foljambe by 1835 when the Foden's son, Thomas, was born after they had moved to Dodworth.

Jeremiah Gilbert would seem to have retained some ongoing connection with the area in the months following the disaster as Silkstone is given as his abode when he was married exactly five months to the day after it had happened.

*Jeremiah Gilbert*
P.M.P
Aged 40 Y[rs]

Portrait of Jeremiah Gilbert
*My Primitive Methodists website*

His bride was 18-year-old Ann Wilkinson, the daughter of
Thomas and Alice Wilkinson from Bolton Percy to the east of
Tadcaster, but the marriage took place at Wickersley, near
Rotherham. Ann had to get used to a rather nomadic
existence for much of her married life but for two years from
1823 the couple were settled in North Shields where her
husband was head missionary. His widowed mother,

Elizabeth, whose well-being his letter following the disaster appears to express some fear for, lived for almost another fourteen years, being buried at St Andrew's, Caunton, during 1835 at the age of eighty-one.

Jeremiah and Ann had at least six children and their individual birthplaces evidence the preacher's travels after his time in the north east of England. Their son, also Jeremiah, was born during October 1826 at Duffield near Belper in Derbyshire and, at the time of the 1841 census, he was lodging with Thomas and Sarah Scofield in High Street, Chesterfield. His sister, Jane, had been born in 1832, when the family were in Shropshire and, after Gilbert had become Superintendent of the town's Primitive Methodist Circuit, Joseph was born in Brampton, Chesterfield during 1837. Ann was born nearly three years later when Gilbert was then based in Burton-upon-Trent. The fact that only his wife and children Jane, Joseph and Ann were recorded at their home in Station Street in the 1841 census suggests that he was still travelling. On census night that year he was staying with a Shrigley family in Doveridge, Uttoxeter, Derbyshire with his occupation noted as "Prim. Minister."

Gilbert's other children, Mary and Thomas, were born in 1844 and 1846 respectively, while the family were firstly in Winster near Matlock and then, Newark close to his Caunton origins. Towards the end of his life, Gilbert was described as a "supernumerary" on the Chesterfield circuit[242] but is recorded in the 1851 census as a "grocer". He was resident then at 1 Bath Terrace, Chesterfield, with his wife, Ann, and five youngest children. Hugh Bourne, widely regarded as a main founding father of the Primitive Methodist movement, died in October the following year aged eighty and Jeremiah Gilbert, his staunch apostle, passed away not long after on 30 December, 1852 at Hasland, to the south of Chesterfield.

# 15.

# Trials, Tribulations
# and Stony Inhumanity

WE TEND to overlook the fact that ordinary working folk in the nineteenth century would have had little alternative but to carry on with life whatever the emotional toll of losing loved ones, alongside the more practical issue of each of those lost being a wage-earner and contributor to the family income. The fact that, within just two decades of the disaster, Upper Norcroft was occupied by an almost totally different community of families underlines the transient lives of so many people at that time. And colliers, in particular, were industrial travellers so very often on the move from area to area following the opportunities for work. It is most likely that the changes happening on the Banks Estate in the years following 1821 may well have had a significant impact upon the local collier families.

How long, if at all, the operation of the Flatlands shaft continued following the 1821 tragedy is not known. It has been recorded that a spoil heap close to the main Norcroft

Colliery was removed in 1826 and there are questions as to whether this main site was actually being run down by then. Charles Pratt notes in that year the "late Vestry Book" for Cawthorne parish church recording the establishment of a committee charged with the task of creating work for the local poor who were without employment. Improvements to the parish highways were recommended by the committee in a report published in November 1826, which also suggested at the western end of Norcroft Lane, "the widening of Woolstocks Lane, from Banks gate to Hill House gate."[243] Pratt refers also to, "the widening of that part of Norcroft Lane which joins the Silkstone Road by removing the Pit Hill..."[244] It is debatable whether the removal of this 'pit hill' necessarily confirmed the closure by then of the main Norcroft Colliery as its apparent location at this junction would suggest it could actually have been the slag heap from the workings of the former Botany Bay pit which was just to the north side of the junction. Nevertheless, both pits were linked underground,[245] were both being worked by Samuel Thorp and it is likely that their operation was closely connected. Photographic evidence exists of a 'pit hill' at Lower Norcroft still in existence well into the twentieth century.

Whether or not the closures had taken place within five or so years of the disaster, it is clearly the case that a considerable amount of the coal resources on the Banks estate had been mined some years before 1826. An accounts statement for Banks Farm with a date which appears to be 1818, notes some ninety-two different closes under Samuel Thorp's name, many of which are listed against the term "coal got". Others are accompanied by the comment "no coal" and one adds "doubtful if coal but clearly not pittable." There is also reference in the statement to "New Pit. Bapit (sic) of Botany Bay half got"[246] indicating a likely reference to

William Mosley and his son, Charles, haymaking at Lower Norcroft
in 1936 with the pit hill clearly visible                    *G. Mosley*

the pit referred to in Thorp's letter of 1814 which had stated
he was 'beginning' near Upper Norcroft.[247] The accounts
statement is further evidence of the location of the disaster
site, referring to "41 Lower Fat Lands" (sic) with close 41
presumably being known as Lower Flatlands.[248]

Although it is difficult to confirm that Norcroft
Colliery was no longer active by 1826, it is clear from archive

evidence that the acreage of Banks being worked by Thorp's colliers, although varying year by year, was gradually reducing.[249] Another factor of relevance to its possible demise is the transfer of the ownership of the Banks land by this time to the nearby Cannon Hall estate. John Goodchild records that Francis Fawkes, the owner of Banks, died during 1818[250] and Thorp, "seems to have carried on his working of the Banks Colliery until 1829, despite the sale of the Banks estate...in 1826."[251] A copy of Thorp's accounts for 1821-22[252], however, suggests that this sale had actually taken place some time before the death of the purchaser, Walter Spencer-Stanhope, in early April 1821.

As far back as 1818 it seems that Thorp had faced financial difficulties, which were intermittent during his mining on the Banks estate. His solicitor George Keir had, in February of that year, referred to the extent of his indebtedness[253] and some of his outgoings over the following decade will have clearly added to his problems. Michaelmas – 29 September – was traditionally the time when half yearly rents were due and, just over four months after the Norcroft tragedy he was required to pay £20 to the Spencer-Stanhopes for four years' use of the rail road over their land.[254] That December, the Cannon Hall accounts record the receipt of "an acceptance from Mr Thorp as two months" of £600 for the estate rental.[255] The estate papers also note a gradual decline in the extent of Spencer-Stanhope land he was working for coal, reducing from just over four acres to just over three between 1824 and 1825.[256] By 1828-29 the area was a little over one acre.[257]

Thorp's rental payments were integral to the operation of his pits and the transporting of coal to Barnby Basin, but the overall picture gained is that it seems he found it challenging to maintain his lifestyle and status. His account with the Spencer-Stanhopes evidences the fact that during April 1822, he was paying the sizeable amount of £250 for just six months' rent of Banks Hall[258] and an inventory on his death suggests an appetite for living well. His alcohol collection included two gallons of whisky, four gallons of gin, three gallons of rum, four gallons of brandy and some 240 bottles of port.[259]

Thorp had made his main will in early 1827 but it is difficult to establish from this and a codicil dated a few weeks later exactly what his personal financial position was by then, particularly in relation to his mining operations. The impression is gained that he certainly had debts requiring cash settlement but the will appears to have offered some possible exemption of his coal interests when it came to his instruction to monetise his personal estate. It clearly accepts the need for their disposal if all the monies raised, "shall not be sufficient to pay, satisfy and discharge all my just debts…"[260] Thorp's first wife had died in 1791, shortly after the birth of their son, Richard. His second wife Mary was to receive a specified annuity of £80 from the proceeds of his business and colliery concerns but the will made clear that this should be paid from what arose from their sale if this was necessary.

The codicil, drafted – like the earlier will – by Keir, implies that a contraction of some of Thorp's local coal interests was already by then underway. It confirmed that he had passed to his son, Samuel Thorp jr., "certain engines, pipes and other colliery implements, for the purpose of winning and working certain coal mines within the Manor of Ardsley."[261] Alongside the signature of Keir witnessing both documents, were the names of his servants, Jno. Gothard and James Barlow on the will and Elizabeth Firth and Frances Taylor on the codicil.[262]

The Jagger family seem to have remained at Norcroft

An aerial view of Upper Norcroft Farm                    *C. Walley*

---

through the changes in the mining of the Banks estate and the
implications of the older Samuel Thorp's death. David Jagger
was living with his wife Elizabeth in the Upper Norcroft
cottages during 1821 and could have been one of the colliers
working underground at the time of the accident. They had
been in Cawthorne during 1815, when daughter Mary was
born but were resident at Norcroft by June 1819, when
Elizabeth gave birth to another girl, Jane. She had their last
child, David, there during August 1830 but he was being
buried towards the end of the following February. That year
– 1831 – was to be another sad one at Norcroft, especially for
the Jaggers. Daughter Ann's illegitimate child, christened
Sarah Ann Birkhead Jagger, had been born a couple of months
before David during the previous summer but also was dead
by the following March, aged just nine months. Her third
Christian name implied paternity being the responsibility of
a member of the neighbouring Birkhead family and Ann had

married John Birkhead at Christmas, 1830. To conclude the losses of that following year, Ann's mother Elizabeth was buried at the end of October, aged forty-two.

While most of the other families previously living in the cottages had moved away, David Jagger's continued in residence and he was still mining locally in 1841. His occupation was again recorded as "coal miner" in the census ten years later where he is living at "51 Cawthorne" with a new wife – Elizabeth – who at twenty-nine was less than half his age. David may have avoided being one of the 1821 casualties but his life was to end when he was one of thirteen victims of the explosion at Higham Colliery near Barnsley in February 1860. In the continuing tradition of collier family teamwork, his sixteen-year-old grandson – another David Jagger – was working with him as a hurrier and also lost his life. Young David was one of two illegitimate sons of Maria Jagger who was recorded as working as a "charwoman", residing at "25 Cawthorne" in 1851, and his putative father at his baptism in 1843 is noted as a George Danforth. Maria's second son, who was born in 1847, was named George and the census return of four years later records a collier of that name living on Taylor Hill, Cawthorne. The two David Jaggers were laid to rest together at Cawthorne on 19 February 1860.

The Jagger family was to have a continuing connection with Thomas Fox, the sole survivor of the Norcroft disaster. David and (the first) Elizabeth Jagger's daughter Mary had given birth to an illegitimate child, also Elizabeth, who was baptised in 1837. She is listed in the 1851 census as residing at the Old Windmill public house at 19 Shambles Street, Barnsley where she was working as a fifteen-year-old "house servant." Fox, by then, was the landlord. His ability to seemingly prosper in later life may have had some connection to the fact that both he and his family had longstanding close associations with the Thorp family. Fox's father, also Thomas, was a glassmaker who was described as being of Silkstone parish when he married Bridget Denton there in 1799. Thomas senior is likely to have been working at Thorp's Gawber Hall glasshouse when his son was born at Gawber during 1805. Young Thomas would have been sixteen years of age at the time of the disaster but it is impossible to establish whether, like most of the Norcroft victims, he had started work many years earlier as a child collier. He could have worked nearer to his place of birth early on in his life, possibly at another of the Thorp pits, as it is clear that glass production at Gawber was declining as he grew older. The estate containing the glasshouse was auctioned off just a few weeks before he was very seriously injured in the incident of May 1821.[263] There is no evidence as to whether Thomas Fox had ever returned to working underground after the accident but bearing in mind that, according to his obituary, "both his arms and one thigh were broken, and he had to remain in bed twelve months,"[264] this must have been very unlikely.

While our contemporary appreciation of the dangers of mining often focuses on the fatalities which occurred it is likely that, during Fox's lifetime, for every collier losing his or her life there would be three or four more seriously injured in the way he was and often permanently disabled. One collier who began work in the mid-1800s summed up the brutal reality of the time in recalling, "Never had I seen so many crutches, so many empty jacket sleeves, so many wooden legs."[265] The rehabilitative support available nowadays following major trauma would have been non-existent then, with life-long incapacity so often the inevitable consequence. Walter Spencer-Stanhope's earlier description of the men guarding the local warning beacon perhaps evidenced this.

Fox's marriage to Sarah Crossland took place at Barnsley St Mary's Church during August of 1827. She seems to have been pregnant with their son James by then and, on his baptism the following February, while Fox was still described as a collier, the likelihood is that he was probably undertaking lighter surface work by then. It seems that he may have left mining altogether by 1841 when the Census of that year recorded his occupation as "labourer". He was then living at Green Foot to the north of Old Town, Barnsley not far from the branch of the Barnsley Canal which ran north west from its junction with the Dearne and Dove Canal towards Barugh Bridge and Barnby Basin.

In accordance with the practice of the time, Thomas Fox's listing at the top of the Census entry, followed by Sarah and thirteen-year-old James gives the impression that he 'headed' the household in 1841 but the next entry down is for thirty-year-old Ann Thorp who is described as 'independent'. It was the requirement then – as now – for the Census record to accurately reflect the detail of those resident at a particular address on the day in question and it would appear that absent from home that day was the man who would, perhaps, otherwise have headed the list of those resident – Samuel Thorp, Ann's husband and the son of the late Banks Hall entrepreneur of the same name, for whom Thomas Fox had been working when he had been so seriously injured in 1821.

The mining historian and prolific writer on Barnsley's history Brian Elliott has explained that the Green Foot area had, at this time, a bleachworks and several old collieries, including the Thorp's Gawber pit. "Weavers and colliers lived in...the more industrial lower part of the area. 'Upper' Green Foot included a few more well to do properties..."[266]

where is it is likely the Foxes lodged with Samuel Thorp junior and his wife, Ann. Of course, the 'division' of both Green Foot and Gawber was later institutionalised by the construction of what we now know as the A635 – the Wilthorpe and Huddersfield roads.

The 1841 census return evidenced that Anne and Samuel Thorp junior's three young daughters and one-year-old son were also living at the Green Foot property with the Fox family, along with fifteen-year-old Elizabeth Thorp. Her origins confirm familial connections between the Thorps and Foxes as she was the illegitimate daughter of Anne Fox, baptised at St Mary's, Barnsley during 1825, with Anne subsequently marrying the Norcroft entrepreneur's son. This Thorp's continued involvement in the coal industry is indicated by his occupation being listed as 'coal master' in the entry for the family in the next census in 1851, when they were living at 1 Elmwood Terrace, Little London, Leeds which in Victorian times would have been deemed one of the more desirable areas of the city.

It is a matter of speculation as to whether Thomas Fox's connection to the Thorp family was of influence in him being able to make the step from manual labour into the licensed trade in Barnsley. The fact that he, Sarah and James were apparently living with them in 1841 suggests a magnanimity towards them which is not very obviously in evidence in respect of most of the other families affected by what had happened two decades earlier. During the following year, Fox was described as a widower when at Tankersley to the south of Barnsley, he married Rebecca Roe. His occupation is given as an engineer and the fathers of both marriage partners are listed as glassmakers.

There would still have been some heavy work during Fox's many years as landlord of the Old Windmill but, as well as the support of his second wife Rebecca, Thomas Fox, had the help of a fifteen-year-old female "house servant" according to the 1861 census. For someone who may well have been significantly disabled by the 1821 accident, he seems to have been able to acquire some wealth during his time in the licensed trade and by the age of sixty-six being able to retire. He appears financially secure, with the 1871 census describing his occupation as an "annuitant". By then they were living not far from the Shambles at 7 Westgate, Barnsley, close to the old police lock-up at number one occupied at the time by Police Superintendent George Sykes and four of his officers.

By the time he died during 1884, Fox had been described in that decade's census as a "Retired Innkeeper (Gentleman)", which might be regarded as quite some advancement for a former collier lad. He had been living at 152 Sheffield Road, Barnsley along with Rebecca and twenty-one-year-old grandson Tom. Fox's son was running the Queen's Hotel in Barnsley at the time of his death but the past links with the coal industry were not completely lost. Young Tom was described in the 1881 census as a "Colliery Traveller," possibly a transcription error for colliery tunneller. A remarkable legacy of the Fox family is the Fox Wing at Barnsley's Cooper Gallery. James Fox's obvious business acumen and wealth gave him the wherewithal to collect works of art and on his death, his son not only passed this collection to the Gallery but also provided the funding to create a new wing there to display the collection.

The family of sixteen-year-old Thomas Blackburn may, some years after the disaster, have been near neighbours of Thomas Fox, close to the centre of Barnsley. Some two decades after his death at Norcroft, his parents Thomas senior and Betty are recorded as living at "Old Town", Barnsley in the 1841 census. Having previously worked as a carpenter,

Thomas had described his occupation then as "wheelwright". A possible explanation of maternal connections being behind young Thomas's burial at Darton is offered by that also being his mother's final resting place during October 1849. Two years later, widower Thomas was residing in Church Street, Barnsley, with his occupation once again being described as a carpenter.

The obituary of Thomas Fox had described the principal event in his life as, "his connection with a deplorable accident" some sixty years earlier[267] but, in the immediate aftermath of that terrible event and following the awful personal losses came what might be regarded as a little good news. For the Eyre and Townend families there was the arrival less than two months after the disaster of a daughter for Charlotte, with her late husband Thomas, recorded as father on the baptismal entry. After what Charlotte had lived through, it is hard to contemplate how she felt about the child's birth at this time, not least with another mouth to feed when the main wage-earner was no longer around. The sister for eighteen-month-old William was named Roseanne after the mother Charlotte had lost when just five years of age. Almost a year later, during July 1822, John and Mary Eyre baptised their tenth child Richard, and consistent with the two year gaps between births, their last son Job in July 1824. The dozen was completed by Elizabeth, born during March 1827.

Most unusually, Elizabeth Eyre wasn't baptised until she was nearly ten but during several of the years following her birth, it is apparent that John, Mary and their substantial family had more pressing matters to address. On 28 April, 1830 the poor law authorities in Cawthorne obtained an order for the removal of the Eyres to Kippax, the parish of John's birth not far off sixty years earlier.[268] Bearing in mind that, less than nine years previously, he had lost his three young sons, his son-in-law and son-in-law's brother in the Norcroft disaster, regardless of the circumstances of the order, this action seems especially harsh even by the standards of the time, particularly as his wife and the six surviving children who had not reached adulthood were all born in Cawthorne.

It would be of some comfort if the Eyres' treatment at this time under the poor law was an isolated example but it wasn't, both locally and elsewhere. W.E. Tate in his classic analysis of parochial administration *The Parish Chest* wrote that the system introduced as far back as 1601 resulted in, "… instances of frequent stony inhumanity, with occasional bestial cruelty to the poor by parish officers…"[269] It might have been hoped that the callous heartlessness of the way families such as theirs were apparently treated in Cawthorne would pave the way for a more humane treatment of the poor but, when the new Whig Government of 1830 replaced local Overseers with Poor Law Unions legislation in 1834, the system was even harsher with the 'outdoor relief' (most probably received by the likes of the Eyres) being largely replaced by a new generation of larger workhouses. Future access to help was to be based on the perceived deterrent effects of destitute families usually being split up on their admission to these degrading institutions.

It is difficult to avoid noting that, as well as living through the remarkable changes of the industrial revolution, the families who feature in the Norcroft story also lived through a period in our history which saw the introduction of what is now regarded as one of the most significant transformations in Britain's social legislation, the 1834 Poor Law Amendment Act. The Napoleonic Wars and the subsequent economic plight of vast numbers in the country in its aftermath had brought things to a head and according to Singleton's examination of the Yorkshire position, "It illustrates the strain which the social changes accompanying the industrial revolution imposed upon an administrative structure devised in Elizabethan England to meet an entirely different set of conditions."[270] Of course, accompanying these rapidly changing circumstances was the view within many parishes that the growing cost of poor relief had to be contained and that preventing what were deemed irresponsible claims for help had to be at the heart of a remodelled Poor Law system.

The options for local families facing hardship at the time were very limited in terms of alternatives to the Poor Law and there would have been, in some instances, a reliance on the charity of the likes of the Spencer-Stanhopes. Their accounts at the start of the nineteenth century, for example, indicate a number of annual payments of 10s. to the schoolmaster of Silkstone "for a poor child."[271] During the years just before the introduction of the so-called New Poor Law, there was some apparent recognition of the need for occasional financial support for women at particular times in their lives. The Cawthorne and Silkstone Benefit Society, established in 1826, made provision solely for females and bearing in mind its trustees constituted those who might be termed local establishment figures, it is possible that a recognition of the need for its formation arose from direct knowledge of the plight of those in the servant class unable to work for various reasons, rather than an awareness of the circumstances of those such as the Eyre family.

The President of the Society was Mrs. Spencer-Stanhope of Cannon Hall and her family were well represented on the Society's committee. J. S. Stanhope, Esq. was its treasurer sitting alongside his brother, Rev. C. S. Stanhope, and the Misses Isabella and Frances Spencer-Stanhope. Rev. R. Affleck, who was Vicar of Silkstone, served alongside two Misses Affleck who were probably his daughters. Among the ten other trustees were Mrs. Thorp and Miss Thorp of Banks Hall. Their role involved all contributing what appear to have been annual subscriptions of 10/6d each, with Mrs Spencer-Stanhope also making a £5.0.0 donation in 1826. The accounts note money also raised by means of bazaars but eligibility for help appears to have been linked to a requirement for prior contributions to the Scheme by any beneficiaries of some three shillings per quarter. Benefit payment columns in the accounts refer to numbers of "weeks bedfast" and "sick/walking" with "Sick Fund" payments – first class – of 2/- per quarter. "Lying-in" payments – second class – were 1/- per quarter.[272]

The likes of the Spencer-Stanhopes and Thorp families were also apparently involved in direct practical benevolence towards the poor, as Anna Maria Wilhelmina Stirling noted in her memoir, *Life's Little Day*. Describing past local custom, she used the term in its original meaning – as a donation to charity – when she noted that, "Both at Cannon Hall and Banks on Christmas Eve the dole was distributed to the poor…" Meat was, "…presented with kindly greeting by the Ladies themselves to each deserving recipient." Her distinction as to the merit or otherwise of those attending for help very much reflected that prevailing within the provisions of the Poor Law at the time, but her comments on the budgetary inadequacies of local collier families suggest some distance from the past realities of their lives. "When the pits stopped work great distress prevailed in the surrounding districts, for the miner in prosperity was an improvident being, and made no provision for a rainy day."[273]

The inability of many families to be able to meet the contributary payments required by the likes of the Cawthorne and Silkstone Benefit Society meant that the circumstances of the likes of the Eyres were unlikely to be addressed. So the threat of this removal order hung over the Eyre family for nearly a year before, on 4 April, 1831 Pontefract Sessions formally confirmed the removal of John, Mary and their six surviving dependent children, Hannah, Joseph, George, James, Job and Eliza from Cawthorne to Kippax.[274] From the fourteenth century, magistrates had been required to hold what came to be known as Quarter Sessions four times each year and their duties had substantially increased by their responsibilities for monitoring the local operation of the system of poor relief. Exactly why the Eyres had become in some way dependent upon the parish around this time is not easy to establish, but might have been related to changes in local coal production which followed the death of the Banks estate entrepreneur Samuel Thorp at his home at Banks Hall in 1829. Any reduction in the earnings of John Eyre around this time would have resulted in him and Elizabeth facing significant problems feeding a sizeable family.

Charlotte's second eldest brother William had, like her, been born in Rothwell and married Sarah Mason in Cawthorne just a few months before the tragedy hit the family. He was a collier then although not referred to in the Gilbert account, and Land Tax returns note him being a Spencer-Stanhope tenant in the village during 1819 and paying rent there to George Hirst during the 1820s. William was still working underground in 1841 when the Cawthorne census return lists him living there with Sarah and two young sons, one of them called Charles most likely in memory of his late brother.

Charlotte herself was to remarry nearly three years after the awful events of 1821 and she and her husband George Garthwaite, a labourer, were to have at least seven children to add to the son and daughter she already had. But, in accordance with the sorrow which seems to have been central to her entire life, Charlotte and her husband lost their first child John in 1829 aged five, their first daughter Fanny in 1833, aged four, and their third son James, in 1836 aged just less than a year. It is simply impossible to imagine what Charlotte had to face in her life. In addition to burying these three children, she lost her mother at the age of five, her eight-year-old brother Thomas during 1810, her four-year-old half-brother James in 1817, her three half-brothers Charles, Robert and Benjamin, her husband William, and brother-in-law John in the 1821 disaster, along with another half-brother Richard in 1830, aged seven.

Charlotte and husband George were still living in Cawthorne in 1841. Residing with their family was twenty-year-old William Townend, born shortly before the Norcroft disaster had taken the lives of his father and four uncles. Two decades on he also was working as a coal miner. The death of a Charlotte Garthwaite is noted in the Barnsley records for 1851 when she would probably have been firty-three. It is difficult to avoid the conclusion that her passing would have been a blessed relief.

Richard Watson's wife Mary appears not to have remarried and was buried at Silkstone aged sixty-six during 1838. Their son Thomas, who would seem to have had the narrowest escapes from death at Norcroft and the terrible experience after sliding down a rope into the shaft, married Hannah Womersley at Silkstone Church just over a year after the tragedy. Their son Richard was most likely named after his grandfather but sadly he only lived for just over a year, being buried just before Christmas 1827. After what Thomas Watson had been through, it would not have been surprising had he moved away from mining, but he is still listed as a "coal miner" in Silkstone in the 1841 census and was in the same occupation ten years later when the family had moved to Blacker Hill, between Worsborough and Hoyland.

Thomas's brother Richard lived at Ardsley, to the east of Barnsley, where his wife Elizabeth came from for some time but, at the time of the 1861 census, is recorded – still working as a coal miner – living with her and their two sons at "Gorse Holes", Worsborough. This is probably Goose Hulls, between Worsborough Dale and Worsborough Bridge. Thomas's place and date of birth in the census is given as Silkstone during 1819 but he was actually born there, to Richard and Mary, in 1812. Very sadly, Richard was to suffer the same fate as his father and die through his work. On 8 December 1862, he was among the fifty-nine fatalities of the explosion at the Edmunds Main colliery at Worsborough Dale.[275]

John Handforth's widow Frances married John Parkinson at Cawthorne church on 30 September 1822. This John, originally from Royston, had also been living at Norcroft and was described as a collier at the time of his first marriage to Mary Green of Cawthorne in September 1814 when she was heavily pregnant with their first child, born just over a month later. John and Mary had two other children before she died aged thirty-six at Norcroft, less than five months after the 1821 disaster.

Perhaps one of the more striking stories of how life moved on is the fact that the son of one of the Norcroft child miners ended up in later life a colliery owner, a freemason and standing in a County Council election for the Conservative Party against the President of the Yorkshire Miners' Association. John Fountain's engagement of at least one of the Townend brothers suggests what might be termed 'entrepreneurial' characteristics within the family. His son George was born in Flockton during the same year as victim John Townend – 1808 - and appears to have had early good fortune by narrowly avoiding being another of the young victims of the 1821 disaster, when he is likely to have been working underground on the Banks estate. Some ten years later he had married Anne Holden, who came from a High Hoyland farming family and seems, as a consequence, to have gradually improved what might be termed his social status. By the 1851 census he was described as a "Coal Miner and Farmer of 20 acres" and alongside Anne and their four children, also living at their home in High Hoyland was a female "House Servant".

An obituary of George and Anne Fountain's son Henry notes that when he left school around 1853 he had gone to work at Haigh Colliery, "which his father had taken a few years before." [276] After George's death in 1871, Henry appears to have joined his brothers in a partnership at this colliery and subsequently became a partner in North Gawber Hall Collieries, previously worked by the Thorps who had also exploited Norcroft. 1889 saw the establishment of the West Riding County Council and Henry Fountain stood as the Conservative candidate in the Darton Division in the authority's first ever elections. He was beaten by just twenty votes by Edward Cowey representing the Yorkshire Miners' Association of which he had been made President during 1876. Fountain, active in Barnsley's Freemasons in later life, died suddenly at the age of fifty during 1892 and, according to the *Barnsley Chronicle*, in addition to being a member of Barnsley Town Council had by then been serving as a member of the County Council representing its Darton Division. [277] The extensive Fountain family colliery interests are explored in some detail in John Goodchild's book, *Coals from Barnsley*. [278]

Just as the background of eight-year-old Charles Forden is something of a mystery, the various spellings of his family name make compiling an accurate account of the continuing life of his family a little challenging. The Cawthorne parish registers record the death during 1825 of

Elizabeth Fording of Norcroft, whose surname is clearly another variant of Charles's and she was most likely to have been this boy's mother. During the following year the records note the marriage of Hannah Moseley to Foljambe Faulding who, in later records, is described as a collier of Norcroft. A Hannah Mosely was recorded in the Cawthorne baptismal records as having given birth to an illegitimate son Henry during March 1815, and she may well have become Foljambe's second wife but obviously the Bastardy Order concerned a child born some years earlier.

Faulding is most likely a further variant of Forden, with Foden subsequently being used in the baptisms of several of Hannah and Foljambe's subsequent children. Their married life clearly faced its difficulties and, during 1833, the couple and their children, John, Sarah and Harriott were also threatened with removal from the parish of Cawthorne, this time to Ecclesfield, under the provisions of the Poor Law. Foljambe had previously had his difficulties with the authorities but it does seem curious that he and his family, like the Eyres, also fell foul of legislation dating back as far as the Act of Settlement of 1601. He had been born in Ecclesfield in 1784 and, under the principles established during the first Elizabethan era, was subject to an attempt to return the family there forcibly when, for whatever reason, he and Elizabeth must have found themselves reliant upon Cawthorne's Overseers of the Poor for 'outdoor relief' in order to survive.

The Overseers dealing with the cases of the Eyres and Fordens at the time were, at least by the very limited standards of that period, subject to a form of local scrutiny, albeit from a rather narrow and select collection of parishioners. The usual practice involved their annual election at a vestry meeting within the church attended by the vicar, churchwardens and prominent parishioners who were likely

**Cawthorne Church:** where vestry meetings oversaw the operation of the local Poor Law
*D. Hinchliffe*

to have been co-opted or elected. It was invariably only men involved in the proceedings during the years before female emancipation and normally a small parish such as Cawthorne appointed a single Overseer who had quite significant responsibilities in what was a voluntary role. He had the ability to raise a local poor rate to raise the funds needed for poor relief within the parish, and was accountable to the vestry meeting for how the money was spent. Bearing in mind that those attending the vestry meeting would normally be contributors to the poor rate, the Overseer is more likely to have been closely questioned over his expenditure on the poor than on the appropriateness of his attempts to remove local families from the area. Reducing the numbers of those reliant upon poor relief would have been a central objective for the Overseer, particularly as he could be held personally liable for payments the vestry meeting did not agree with.

During the years following the Norcroft disaster, from 1822 Walter Spencer-Stanhope's son Charles was the Cawthorne incumbent and his successor, Charles Pratt, has made clear in his history of the parish[279] that a 'close' or 'select' vestry system was used at the time, with co-option of representatives being the norm. Pratt's quotes from the Vestry Book of the period evidence that the meetings to which the Overseer would report were chaired by Rev. Spencer-Stanhope or his brother John, the occupant of Cannon Hall following Sir Walter's death. As well as outlining the extent to which the unemployed were required to undertake work such as breaking stones to qualify for relief during the 1820s, Pratt says of the Cawthorne Vestry Book, "Frequent mention is made of loans to the poor 'towards the payment of their rent'".[280] Bearing in mind that, according to the Land Tax Returns for this period, the Spencer-Stanhope family were the main landlords in the area at this time, it seems that potential conflicts over pecuniary interests were perhaps less of an issue then than in later years. Their own accounts from the year of the Norcroft tragedy evidence the receipt of rent from almost eighty properties just within Cawthorne, together with amounts from tenants further afield.

These same accounts, however, also suggest that the Spencer-Stanhopes did contribute substantially towards provision for the poor in the local area. Just a week after the disaster on their land in 1821 their records note for May 31, "By John Livesley for a poor assessment for Cannon Hall £19.8.9d, for Dean Hill £3.14.4 ½d."[281] Dean Hill was the family property between the Hall and High Hoyland village. Livesley himself was one of the Spencer-Stanhopes many tenants and, as churchwarden, is recorded also being in receipt of 5s. on the following day for "11 church briefs", charitable contributions usually arising from a royal mandate and in support of a particular cause. And Livesley, as the likely Overseer, is recorded as being paid £5.5s. for what it described as "Three towns cottages."[282] This payment indicates the Spencer-Stanhopes may have paid for the maintenance of three properties in Cawthorne for the accommodation of the poor.

The law was quite clear at the time in requiring the return of paupers to the original parish of the 'head' of the household. Court records show that the Foden's removal order was made at Wakefield on 18 December 1833 at the behest of the Cawthorne Overseers, was contested by those of Ecclesfield and an order at Doncaster Quarter Sessions on 8 January, 1834, discharged the original order for their removal made less than a month earlier. The case appears to be a classic example of what Tate describes as, "…the colossal volume of litigation between parishes…"[283] which had arisen over disputes about the responsibility of Overseers for dependent individuals and families. It is unclear whether the family were actually within Ecclesfield parish during the Christmas of 1833 but Hannah and Foljambe were living in Dodworth when Thomas, probably their fourth child, was born during 1836. Three years later, they appear to have settled at Fall Head in Silkstone parish when another son William was born. Foljambe was still working as a miner but the surname is recorded with a previously used variant, the latest child being named Fording. It seems that Foljambe died during 1841, with an Ecclesfield burials entry for Folgambe Fawden. The widowed Hannah was still at Fall Head when the 1851 census records the surname of her and her children as Folden.

Benjamin Hinchliffe, born at Upper Norcroft in 1827     *D. Hinchliffe*

Foljambe's period at Norcroft coincided with a time where the prime era of Banks estate coal production had most likely passed, and it is a distinct possibility that his family's destitution during 1833 was the result of a marked reduction in colliery employment in that area around this time. He may have had no work at all or been forced to seek some augmentation of his reduced income from the parish. It will have been little consolation to the family that, during the following year, after the election of a Whig Government in 1830, the system of 'outdoor relief' which had supported workers facing hard times was abolished and replaced with a much harsher approach with "the Poor Law Bastilles"[284] workhouse system at its heart.

The Hinchliffe family remained living at Norcroft until well into the 1830s when, following the death of Samuel Thorp, it is obvious that the era of Norcroft coal was in decline. Jehoshaphat and Mary had further sons born in 1823 and 1825 as well as my great-grandfather, Benjamin, during late 1827.

William and Ann Hinchliffe's next to last child, Emma had been born less than two months before Benjamin and her baptism along with that of her next oldest sibling, Ann in early 1824 suggests they could have left Norcroft by then - the parental abodes for both being recorded as Cawthorne, and they were living at Barnby Furnace in 1841. When Frederick and Mary Hinchliffe had their son, also Frederick, baptised at Cawthorne Church in June 1832, he was still working as a collier and living at Norcroft but the family's time here was coming to an end. During August of the following year, having lost his wife Mary almost ten years earlier during 1823, John Hinchliffe – most likely the father of Frederick and Jehoshaphat – died at the age of eighty-five. He had been described as a collier just before Jehoshaphat was born, well over forty years earlier and is quite likely to have been a child collier decades before that. While it is right to be cautious over what is noted in the records of this period, his survival to obviously a good age, having undoubtedly had the toughest of lives, is nothing short of extraordinary during an era when average life expectancy was half that.

As the old collier's life came to an end, so did the Thorp family's lengthy involvement with exploiting the coal reserves of the Banks estate. Earlier in the summer of 1833,

Richard Thorp had written to Thomas Spencer-Stanhope at Cannon Hall giving notice of the intention to surrender possession of all the land and premises they held at Norcroft and Banks by February of the following year.[285] By this time it is clear that a significant proportion of the estate's coal reserves had been mined, with its extraction having been completed in most of the ninety-two 'closes' listed under Samuel Thorp's name.[286] But it is worth noting that, of the eighteen families and 110 people recorded as living at Upper Norcroft in 1841, seven were still involved in mining, including that of twenty-five-year-old Mary Popplewell, one of the remaining women colliers whose work underground would be banned by legislation the following year.

The changes taking place on and around the Banks estate will have impacted upon those who had been working at its various pits, so it is not surprising to note Jehoshaphat Hinchliffe was living and most likely working in Dodworth when daughter Ellen was born shortly before Christmas 1833. The name given to this child is possibly further evidence of a fraternal relationship between Jehosaphat and Frederick Hinchliffe, whose fifteen-year-old daughter Ellen had died three years earlier. A familial relationship with William Hinchliffe also seems likely as he and his wife had baptised their new daughter with the same name not long after the death.

Frederick and his wife Mary clearly never forgot their loss and baptised their last child Ellen. She was born in Lancashire during 1837 as the family had been living over the Pennines in Ashton-under-Lyne for at least three years by then. Although the 1841 census records that Frederick was still working as a coal miner, it is open to question whether it was work opportunities in the cotton industry which actually drew them over there. Their three eldest children were cotton winders, weavers and piecers respectively, living with them at the home in Waterloo Buildings, Ashton, they shared with a Gallagher family, originally from Ireland. Waterloo is located to the north west of the town and an 1848 map of the area notes the nearby Lime Hurst Colliery where Frederick is likely to have worked.[287] The local mills employing the Hinchliffe children would have used locally mined coal and the opening of the Ashton Canal in 1796 had significantly increased demand for it to fuel the huge expansion of the cotton industry taking place in Manchester. Frederick's first wife Mary appears to have died during the early 1840s, as he is married to Mary Ann McKan at St Michael's Church, Ashton-under-Lyne in 1845.

In the baptismal register entry for Jehoshaphat's daughter in 1833, Ellen's mother is noted as 'Hannah' but the name had reverted to Mary Hinscliff (sic) by the time she was recorded living at "Bottom Off (sic) The Flags", Churwell – between Morley and Leeds – in the 1841 census. As was the case on the other side of the Pennines, the need for coal in the expanding steam powered local textile industry drew mining families like the Hinchliffes to the area. At the time of the census, as well as Jehoshaphat working in a local pit, their three teenage sons were employed as coal hurriers and twenty-year-old daughter as a coal dresser, involved with its cleaning at the surface.

Jehoshaphat had survived in one of the most dangerous occupations for around half a century but the death certificate of "Joseph Hinchcliffe, Coal Miner" – who I believe was him – showed he passed away in Churwell on 18 August 1849 as a result of "Malignant Cholera"[288] which is noted to have killed upwards of twenty people locally by the second week that month.[289]

Compared to others in the area who were widowed

at this time, Mary was fortunate to have children of working age ensuring some family income, but the daughter of the same name – born in Norcroft back in 1919 – was, by the time 1819 of the 1851 census, in apparently reduced circumstances. This Mary was listed living in the Poor House at Churwell working as a washerwoman. Jane, the oldest of her three illegitimate children residing with her, was already working at the age of nine as a 'piecener' in the local textile industry. The job was not as dangerous as those of her Norcroft relatives at a similar young age but, in assisting adult spinners, would still involve crawling under working machines to retrieve fallen wool.

Jehoshaphat's widow Mary had collier sons, Jonas and Benjamin, still living at the family home on "Road Side, Churwell", what is now Elland Road. According to the census, their home was on the opposite side of the main road to nearby St. Peter's Church where Jehoshaphat was buried, and close to the former Old Golden Fleece Inn. That pub, on the main Elland Road, was demolished around 2011 and is now the site of a Tesco store.[290] While her youngest daughter Ellen, seventeen, was – like Jane – working in the textile industry as a cloth burler, Mary's occupation was at this time given as "shop keeper" and it is likely she was selling produce from her own house. Towards the end of his life, when he was no longer mining coal in the Normanton area, near Wakefield, Benjamin also dealt in groceries from his house in Elsicker Lane, Warmfield, as did his collier son Oliver from Woodbine Cottage at nearby Heath in his later years.

Perhaps it is entirely appropriate that this Norcroft account should end with Oliver Hinchliffe, my grandfather. It was his older sister, Clara Abigail Ladlow, whose daughter "Auntie" May, started me out on this extraordinary journey in the first place.

**16.**

# The Sound of
# Profitable Commerce

AFTER A detailed exploration of what the 1821 Norcroft pit disaster meant for the local community and for the families directly affected, it genuinely saddens me to say that in terms of national – and even local – significance, the accident scarcely raised an eyebrow.

I have found no records of any expressions of regret, condolence or offers of support and assistance to those such as Charlotte Townend, whose world would have been turned completely upside down.

The archive materials which do exist from the estate of the entrepreneur operating the pit – Samuel Thorp of Banks Hall – appear to include no mention whatsoever of what happened on 23 May 1821. And while the Spencer-Stanhope family, who had become the owners of the Banks estate by 1820, would have been experiencing their own grief at the loss of patriarch Walter just a few weeks earlier, some possible acknowledgement of this sad event, which might have been expected, has also been impossible to find within their surviving family records.

In what is otherwise a quite detailed account of the significant events of the time in the wider locality of Barnsley, while John Hugh Burland wrote extensively of Spencer-Stanhope's passing and also noted that of Cannon Hall agent John Howson during 1821, the deaths of the Norcroft ten that May merited no mention at all.

This examination of the detailed circumstances of what happened two centuries ago raises particular questions as to why, at a time when serious efforts were being made to abolish the international slave trade and, at a domestic leve, measures were being introduced for the protection of minors, particularly in factory employment, there was no apparent outcry of any sort about the ages of the Norcroft victims. William Wilberforce, deemed the architect of slavery's abolition, would have been warmed by Banks estate coal during his occasional visits to Cannon Hall but like so many of his political contemporaries, appears silent regarding the nature of the lives of working children living nearby. As his friend Walter Spencer-Stanhope's burial record faces that of young John Hinchliffe for posterity, it is paradoxical to observe that it was said Wilberforce used to write to him at Cannon Hall for information relating to, "the situation of our labouring poor – a matter of the first importance in political economy."[291] Used in the context of the slave trade, one account of his life included phrases equally applicable to the Cawthorne of 1821: "The sound of profitable commerce effectively silenced ethical and religious scruples..."[292] Putting it even more bluntly "economics simply trumped morality."[293]

Strikingly, Frank Machin's landmark work *The Yorkshire Miners: a history*, has only the very briefest of mentions that in May 1821, "an accident occurred at a colliery at Silkstone, near Barnsley...(when) eleven men were ascending..."[294] Even a book as highly regarded as this in recording the many struggles of mining communities makes no reference to the fact that eight of these 'men' were aged sixteen or younger and two only eight-years-old. Reflecting on the sparse coverage of such tragedies in the newspapers of the time, John Threlkeld's conclusion was that they were largely irrelevant to daily life. "These news items were often relegated to the depths of newspaper columns, indicating that in the view of the Editor – and therefore the public – they were frequent and minor incidents."[295]

It has been particularly noticeable, in studying the area's industrial history during the late eighteenth and early nineteenth centuries, that the fatal accident involving seven victims which occurred over fifteen years earlier at nearby Barnby Furnace Colliery in 1805, seems to have had considerably more impact upon the public consciousness than what happened at Norcroft. Joseph Wilkinson, in his *Notes and Cuttings relating to Silkstone and Dodworth* wrote that following the Barnby tragedy, "...the deceased were followed to their last resting place by large and deeply sympathising numbers. To perpetuate such a fearful loss of life a memorial stone was placed in the churchyard at Cawthorne where the men were buried."[296]

It has been suggested that this memorial – provided by public subscription - is the oldest existing one to a mining accident in the South Yorkshire area.[297] Until the erection during 2019 of the memorial to the Norcroft victims in Cawthorne churchyard, just a few yards away from the Barnby one, the complete absence of any formal acknowledgement of their sacrifice has been extraordinary, especially as there had been more fatalities in the 1821

IN
MEMORY OF

THE TEN MEN AND BOYS
KILLED IN THE NORCROFT COLLIERY DISASTER
23RD MAY 1821

THE FOLLOWING WERE BURIED IN THIS CHURCHYARD
IN AN UNMARKED GRAVE

CHARLES EYRE, TIVEY-DALE, AGED 16
ROBERT EYRE, TIVEY-DALE, AGED 12
BENJAMIN EYRE, TIVEY-DALE, AGED 10
CHARLES FORDEN, NORCROFT, AGED 8
JOHN HINCHLIFFE, NORCROFT, AGED 8
JOHN TOWNEND, CAWTHORNE, AGED 13
THOMAS TOWNEND, CAWTHORNE, AGED 23

MAY THEY NEVER BE FORGOTTEN
REST IN PEACE

**Norcroft memorial:** Julia and David Hinchliffe at the memorial at its dedication on 23 May 2019                   *D. Hinchliffe*

accident and which had also involved children. But Barnby perhaps had, it has been suggested, the distinction of recording the first deaths from a gas explosion within the region[298] and is known to have resulted in significant changes in underground ventilation systems insisted upon by the workforce there before the pit reopened.[299]

Strange as it may seem, with the increased awareness of the dangers from gas, fatalities arising from more easily rectifiable causes might have been deemed a relative 'success'. Rev. W. Thorp later recorded that his father Samuel Thorp had, between 1802 and 1829, worked locally, "above 300 acres of highly inflammable Silkstone coal, without a single accident from explosion."[300] In an era where such explosions commonly caused multiple fatalities perhaps this was a not insignificant achievement, albeit of scant consolation to those dying below Flatlands.

In trying to understand the relative 'insignificance' of the loss of the Norcroft lives compared to Barnby, there appears to be no evidence of any similarly enduring impact of what happened in 1821. If there were consequent changes in shaft practices arising from any lessons which may have been learned from the accident, they appear to have been of only limited value as at other pits not far from Cawthorne, fatalities continued to occur some still involving children. Machin records the death of a boy in 1856 at a colliery near Wakefield when the hempen rope, still in use by then, snapped with him being, "precipitated to the bottom of the shaft and killed."[301] But by then a formal system of mines inspection was in place offering some limited safeguards, and the pit's owner was subject to prosecution and fined. Nevertheless, shaft accidents continued elsewhere in the West Riding with four men being killed some two years later at Killamarsh Pit to the south east of Sheffield, when rope again being used to pull the lift cage snapped. An inquest later held at the local Navigation Inn found the rope concerned had been damaged, having been burned in a small fire during the previous day.[302] North of Killamarsh, at Thryberg Hall

Colliery to the east of Rotherham, six men and boys were killed in another shaft accident when the 'chair' they were using to descend overturned and they fell 150 yards to the bottom.[303] Nearer to Cawthorne and Silkstone, the Wharncliffe Silkstone Colliery at Pilley, south of Barnsley saw two shaft accidents caused by the breaking of a rope within the space of a year. Three men were killed descending the pit when the rope snapped on 30 November 1865 and another three in a similar incident during the following year.[304]

Living at Warmfield near Wakefield by then, Benjamin Hinchliffe would have been especially aware of the eight fatalities when a cage fell at Victoria Colliery, Snydale not far from his home during 1879, as he had lived there during 1854 when his son John was born. We will never know if he had any awareness of what had happened at Norcroft, his birthplace, just six years before he began his life. But, if he had, it would have been interesting to know his feelings when, over sixty years on from the Flatlands tragedy, there were exactly the same number of fatalities when a cage dropped to the shaft bottom as they were ascending at Houghton Main Colliery, Darfield near Barnsley.[305]

If there is any comfort to be drawn from this collection of just some of the continuing shaft fatalities, it is in the fact that the casualty lists can be gradually seen to feature less children. While it is shameful that there appear to have been no serious steps taken to prevent this continuing toll of lives lost, it is perhaps even more deplorable that, following Norcroft, there was no significant consideration of the appropriateness of employing children underground until the profound repercussions of the deaths of twenty-six youngsters in the Husker disaster at Silkstone Common, nearly seventeen years later. There is little doubt that many of those whose lives were lost that day – and their families –

would have been known to those connected to the earlier tragedy of 1821. It is particularly sad that William Hinchliffe's wife Ann, who would have been obviously affected by the death of young John Hinchliffe of Norcroft in 1821, was also to lose her niece Sarah Newton in the Husker tragedy at exactly the same age of just eight years. Ann's sister Martha Newton (née Youel) was the little girl's mother.[306]

Compared to Husker, Norcroft was indeed of limited consequence historically and in terms of the totality of its victims was negligible alongside the hundreds who were to be killed – sometimes in single incidents – at various local collieries later in the nineteenth century and beyond.

Yet Britain's industrial revolution would never have happened without the mining of coal and, in accepting its enduring impact upon the way we live, it is vitally important to bear in mind those individuals who gave their lives to make it happen. For far too many of them, those lives were often very short. Like that of eight-year-old John Hinchliffe, my almost certain relative.

# Bibliography

Addy, J. *A Coal and Iron Community in the Industrial Revolution*. Longman, 1986.

Bardsley, A. *First Name Variants*. Federation of Family History Societies, 2003.

Barker, P. *Yorkshire Villages*. Parkgate, 1998.

Baines, E. *Baines's Yorkshire, Vol. 1*. David and Charles, 1969.

Best, N. *Trafalgar*. Wiedenfield and Nicolson, 2005.

Burland, J. H. *Annals of Barnsley and its Environs, vol 1, 1744-1830*. (Barnsley Archives).

Chase, M. S. *1820: Disorder and Stability in the United Kingdom*. Manchester U. P., 2015.

Cruickshank, J. L. *Headingley-cum-Burley c1540-c1784*. Thoresby Society, 2012.

Day, M. *Wool and Worsit*. Laverock, 2013.

Dransfield, J.N. *A History of the Parish of Penistone*. James H. Wood, 1906.

Elliott, B. (ed.) *Aspects of Barnsley, 2*. Wharncliffe, 1994.

Elliott, B. (ed.) *Aspects of Barnsley, 4.* Wharncliffe, 1996.

Elliott, B. (ed.) *Aspects of Barnsley, 5.* Wharncliffe, 1998.

Elliott, B. *Coalminers.* Pen and Sword, 2015.

Elliott, B. *South Yorkshire Mining Disasters, vol. 1.*
Pen and Sword, 2006.

Elliott, B. *Tracing Your Coalmining Ancestors.*
Pen and Sword, 2014.

Felling, K. *A History of England.* Macmillan, 1959.

Fisher, P. J. *The Politics of Sudden Death:* The *Office and Role of
the Coroner in England and Wales, 1726-1888.* Unpublished
Leicester University PhD thesis, 2007.

Gallop, A. *Victoria's Children of the Dark.* History Press, 2010.

Gardner, J. and Wenborn, N. (eds.) *The History Today
Companion to British History.* Collins and Brown, 1995.

Goodchild, J. *Coals from Barnsley.* Wakefield Historical
Publications, 1986.

Goodchild, J. *Coal Kings of Yorkshire.* Wakefield Historical
Publications, 1978.

Griffin, A. R. *The Collier.* Shire, 1982.

Hargreaves, J. A. and Haigh, E. A. H. (eds.) *Slavery in
Yorkshire.* University of Huddersfield, 2012.

Hey, D. *The Oxford Guide to Family History.* Oxford
University Press, 1993.

Hey, D. *A History of Penistone and District.* Wharncliffe, 2002.

Hinchliffe, J. *Light on a Hill.* Quacks, York, 2012.

Hobsbawn, E. J. *Labouring Men.* Wiedenfield and Nicolson,
1964.

Horn, P. *Labouring Life in the Victorian Countryside.* Gill and
Macmillan, 1976.

Hunter, J. *South Yorkshire, vols. 1 and 2.* Nichols, 1828.
Republished by E.P., 1974.

Jackson, B. (ed.) *All Saints Church, Cawthorne 1880-1990: One
Hundred Years Since Renovation.* 1980.

Jackson, B. *Cawthorne 1790-1990*. Cawthorne Victoria Jubilee Museum, 1991.

Lake, F. and Preece, R. *Voices From The Dark: Women and Children in Yorkshire Coal Mines.* Yorkshire Mining Museum Publications, 1992.

Longmate, N. *Milestones in Working Class History*. BBC, 1975.

Machin, F. *The Yorkshire Miners: a history. Vol. 1*. National Union of Mineworkers, 1958.

Martin, E. W. *The Shearers and the Shorn*. Routledge and Kegan Paul, 1965.

Maurice, W. *A Pitman's Anthology*. James and James, 2004.

Metropolitan Borough of Barnsley. *Cannon Hall: A Country House Museum*. Undated.

McLeod, H. *Religion and the Working Class in Nineteenth Century Britain*. Macmillan, 1984.

Morgan, K. O. (ed.) *Oxford Popular History of England*. Oxford University Press, 1984.

Morton, A. L. *A People's History of England*. Lawrence and Wishart, 1976.

Pratt, C. T. *A History of Cawthorne*. 1882. On-line source.

Prince, J. F. *The Parish of Silkstone*. Wood, 1922.

Redmonds, G. *A History of Yorkshire Surnames*. Shaun Tyas, 2015.

Redmonds, G. *Christian Names in Family History*. National Archives, 2005.

Redmonds, G. *A Vocabulary of Coal Mining in Yorkshire, 1250-1850*. Northern Mine Research Society, 2016.

Roberts, R. A. *The Clarkes of Silkstone and their Colliers*. Workers' Educational Association, 1979.

Sale, K. *Rebels Against the Future*. Addison-Wesley, 1995.

Singleton, F. *Industrial Revolution in Yorkshire*. Dalesman, 1970.

Smith, P.L. *The Aire And Calder Navigation*. Wakefield Historical Publications, 1987.

Smith, W. *Morley Ancient and Modern*. Forgotten Books, undated.

Stirling, A. M.W. *Annals of a Yorkshire House, vols 1 and 2*. Lane, 1911.

Stirling, A.M.W. *Life's Little Day*, Thornton Butterworth, 1925.

Sykes, G. N. *Silkstone Ancient and Modern*. Self-published, 1976.

Tate, W. E. *The Parish Chest*. Phillimore, 1983.

Taylor, K. *The Making of Wakefield 1801-1900*. Wharncliffe, 2008.

Thompson, E. P. *The Making of the English Working Class*. Penguin, 1981.

Threlkeld, J. *Pits 2*. Wharncliffe, 1989.

Turton, K. *A Grim Almanac of South Yorkshire*. History Press, 2010.

Wain, K. *The Coal Mining Industry of Barnsley, Rotherham and Worksop*. Amberley Publishing. (Kindle edition, 2014).

Yorke, S. *The Industrial Revolution Explained*. Countryside Books, 2017.

# Notes

[1] This transcription reproduces the exact spellings used on the memorial.

[2] Sp. St. 60614. All Spencer-Stanhope archive material referenced 'Sp. St.' is held at Barnsley Archives.

[3] Barnsley Independent, 31 May, 1884, Barnsley Archives..

[4] Behr, R. "Brexit left the elite unharmed", Guardian, 20 January, 2021.

[5] Stirling, A.M.W. "Annals of a Country House."

[6] Sp. St. 60551.

[7] Barnsley MBC. "Cannon Hall: a Country House."

[8] Sp.St. 60549/180.

[9] Sp. St. 60549/186.

[10] Sp. St. 60549/158/159.

[11] Sp. St. 60550/297.

[12] Sp. St. 60657.

[13] Letter to author from Anne Wilkinson, 3 March, 2020.

[14] The cottage, which still exists near to the junction of the A635 Wakefield-Doncaster road with Neil Fox Way, is recorded on some old maps as "Ivy Cottage".

[15] Sp. St. 60684/33 contains a reference to "an ash tree out of Greaves Fold."

[16] 1841 census.

[17] Leeds Intelligencer, 28 May, 1821. Leeds Central Library.

[18] Ibid.

[19] Iris Sheffield Advertiser, 29 May, 1821. Sheffield Archives.

[20] Leeds Intelligencer, op cit.

[21] Thompson, E.P. "The Making of the English Working Class."

[22] Gilbert, J. "Extracts from journals, camp-meetings, revivals etc.", 1824. "My Primitive Methodists" web-site. Internet source.

[23] Thompson, op cit.

[24] Gilbert, op cit.

[25] Ibid.

# Descent into Silence

[26] Barnsley Times and Yorkshire Gazette, 29 January, 1876, Barnsley Archives.
[27] Stirling, op cit.
[28] Ibid.
[29] See Glister, R. in Elliott, B. (ed.) "Aspects of Barnsley 4".
[30] See Taylor, K. "The Making of Wakefield 1801-1900."
[31] See Hey, D. "A History of Penistone and District,"2002.
[32] Pratt, C.T. "A History of Cawthorne."
[33] Sheffield Mercury and Hallamshire Advertiser, 7 July, 1838.
[34] Redmonds, G. "Christian Names in Local and Family History," 2004.
[35] See Cruickshank, J.L. "Headingley-cum-Burley c1540-c1784".
[36] Email to author 4 February, 2021.
[37] Sp. St. 60564/997.
[38] Cole, G.D.H. and Postgate, R. "The Common People".
[39] Stirling, op cit.
[40] Ibid.
[41] House of Commons Hansard, 9 March, 1804.
[42] See Stirling, op cit, and Taylor, H. in "Aspects of Barnsley 5".
[43] Best, P. "Trafalgar."
[44] House of Commons Hansard, 24 June, 1806.
[45] Quoted in Horn, P. "Labouring Life in the Victorian Countryside."
[46] Stirling, op cit.
[47] Chase, M. "1820".
[48] Rix, M. quoted in Singleton, F. "Industrial Revolution in Yorkshire".
[49] Barker, P. "Yorkshire Villages".
[50] Sp. St. 60378/196.
[51] Stirling, op cit.
[52] Ibid.
[53] Yorke, S. "The Industrial Revolution Explained."
[54] Redmonds, G. "The Vocabulary of Coal Mining in Yorkshire, 1250-1850", 2016.
[55] Sp. St. 60609/47.
[56] British Coal Authority map no. 10322.
[57] Sp. St. 60579.
[58] Sp. St. 60609.
[59] Ibid.
[60] Singleton, op cit.
[61] Morton, A.L. "A People's History of England."
[62] Sp. St. 60579/8.
[63] Ibid.
[64] Sp. St. 60579/17.
[65] Smith, P.L. "The Aire and Calder Navigation."
[66] Conversation with author, 27 January, 2021.
[67] Redmonds, G. "A Dictionary of Yorkshire Surnames," 2015.
[68] Sp. St. 60313.
[69] Hunter, J. "South Yorkshire" Vol. 1.
[70] Select Land Tax Records, West Yorkshire Archives.
[71] Sp. St. 60544.

[72] Select Land Tax Records, West Yorkshire Archives.

[73] National Archives IR 1/24f41, IR 1/26f21 and IR 1/29f116.

[74] Redmonds, 2015, op cit.

[75] Pratt, op cit.

[76] Ibid.

[77] Hey, D. "Oxford Guide to Family History," 1993.

[78] EM 1647, Sheffield Archives.

[79] Pratt, op. cit.

[80] Exchequer Court of York at Doncaster, 21 May, 1778, West Yorkshire Archives.

[81] Sp. St. 60544/12.

[82] Sp. St. 60544/8.

[83] Barker, M. "The strange sisters of Banks Hall," in Yorkshire Journal, Summer, 1999.

[84] Redmonds, 2015, op cit.

[85] Stirling, op cit.

[86] Singleton, op cit.

[87] Sp. St. 60657/3-7.

[88] Sp. St. 60564/912.

[89] Sp. St. 60657/3-7.

[90] Ibid.

[91] Select Land Tax Records, West Yorkshire Archives.

[92] Roberts, R.A. "The Clarkes of Silkstone and their colliers."

[93] Goodchild, J. "Coals from Barnsley," 1986.

[94] Bardsley, A. "First Name Variants."

[95] Wilson of Broomhead MSS, Sheffield Archives.

[96] Hugh Polehampton has drawn attention to this mistranslation. Email to author, 17 February, 2021.

[97] Email communication with author, 17 February, 2021.

[98] See "The Tate Family of Gawber" in barnsleyartonyourdoorstep.org.uk

[99] Sp. St. 60657/3-7.

[100] Polehampton, H. in Barnsley FHS "Moving Lives."

[101] This information is contained within the John Goodchild Collection which was being catalogued at the time of writing by West Yorkshire Archives.

[102] Goodchild, J. in Elliott, B. (ed.) "Aspects of Barnsley 2".

[103] Hey, D., 1993. Op cit.

[104] Staincross Militia MSS, John Goodchild Collection, West Yorkshire Archives.

[105] Select Land Tax Records, West Yorkshire Archives.

[106] Smith, D.J. "Aspects of Life in Old Cawthorne."

[107] Pratt, op. cit.

[108] Sp. St. 60699.

[109] Select Land Tax Records, West Yorkshire Archives.

[110] Sp. St. 60699..

[111] Prince, J.J. "The Parish of Silkstone."

[112] Sp. St. 60609/3.

[113] Sp. St. 60579/23.

[114] Teasedale, G. H. "Silkstone Coal". Unpublished notes, 1901, held by National Coal Mining Museum for England.

[115] British Coal Authority map 10322.

[116] Goodchild, 1986, op cit.

[117] Sp. St. 60584/22.

[118] I am particularly grateful to David Flack for drawing attention to the involvement of Blenkinsop at Banks.

[119] Hawley, G. "Norcroft Colliery Disaster, 1821". Internet source.

[120] Elliott, B. "South Yorkshire Mining Disasters", Vol. 1., 2006.

[121] Sp. St. 60579/23.

[122] Dictionary of National Biography, Vol. 40, 1894. Internet source.

[123] British Museum, Biog. 39920. Internet source.

[124] Jackson, B. "Cawthorne 1790-1990."

[125] 1839 Index to Death Duty Registers. Internet source.

[126] "Russia expert in search for paintings," Yorkshire Post, 8 March, 1999.

[127] Barnsley Art On Your Doorstep, "The Hidden Artists of Barnsley."

[128] Redmonds, op cit.

[129] Barnsley Independent, 31 May, 1884, Barnsley Archives.

[130] Sp. St. 60609/5.

[131] Sp. St. 60564/1126.

[132] Burland's Annals of Barnsley.

[133] Ibid.

[134] Wilson, D. in "BBC History", Vol. 9, 2 February, 2007.

[135] Morgan, K.O. "The Oxford Popular History of Britain."

[136] Chase, op cit.

[137] Feiling, K. "A History of England."

[138] Sp. St. 60657/3-7.

[139] Recorded in Cawthorne baptismal registers 1808-1828.

[140] Sp. St. 60654/945.

[141] Sp. St. 60654/100.

[142] Sp. St. 60564/1017.

[143] Sp. St. 60657/7.

[144] Morton, op cit.

[145] Ibid.

[146] Smith, D.J. op cit.

[147] Sp. St. 60564/973.

[148] Sp. St. 60564/975.

[149] Ibid.

[150] Cole and Postgate, op cit.

[151] Sp. St. 60564/1081.

[152] Sp. St. 60564/1071.

[153] Sp. St. 60564/1112.

[154] Hey, 1993, op cit.

[155] Held by Heritage Silkstone.

[156] See Spensley, R. in "Moving Lives".

[157] Copy of National Archives document (NA) CO 48/43, held by Heritage Silkstone.

[158] Ibid.

[159] Ibid.

[160] Hey, 1993, op cit.

[161] Barker, op cit.

[162] Stirling, op cit.

[163] Sp. St. 60657/3-7.

[164] Gardiner, J. and Wenborn, N. "History Today Companion to British History."

[165] Singleton, op cit.

[166] Children's Employment Commission, 1842.

[167] Morton, op cit.

[168] Threlkeld, J. "Pits 2".

[169] Ibid.

[170] Sp. St. 60657/3-7.

[171] Hugh Polehampton has noted that the Thorp family's high regard for Sutcliffe, who was working for them by 1818, if not earlier, is evidenced by their erection of his tomb at Silkstone Church in 1858. Email to author 17 February, 2021.

[172] Roberts, op cit.

[173] Ibid.

[174] Ibid.

[175] Ibid.

[176] Threlkeld, op cit.

[177] Redmonds, 2016, op cit.

[178] Elliott, B. "Coalminers," 2015.

[179] Burland, op cit.

[180] Stirling, op cit.

[181] See Freese, B. "Coal: a Human History."

[182] Sp.St. 60684/1-4.

[183] Machin, F. "The Yorkshire Miners," Vol. 1.

[184] McLeod, H. "Religion and the Working Class in Nineteenth Century Britain."

[185] Gilbert, op cit.

[186] Ibid.

[187] Thompson, op cit.

[188] Hinchliffe, J. "Light on a Hill."

[189] Dews, D.C. in Hargreaves, J.A. and Haigh, E.A.H. (eds.) "Slavery in Yorkshire."

[190] Spensley, R. in Barnsley FHS Journal, Vol.16, No. 3, July, 2008.

[191] Ibid.

[192] Colls, R. "The Collier's Rant."

[193] Ibid.

[194] Ibid.

[195] Ibid.

[196] McLeod, op cit.

[197] Thompson, op cit.

[198] Chase, op cit.

[199] Ibid.

[200] Burland, op cit.

[201] Ibid.

[202] Ibid.

[203] Ibid.

[204] Chase, op cit.

[205] Ibid.

[206] Leeds Mercury, 15 April, 1820. Leeds Central Library.

[207] Ibid.

[208] Ibid.

[209] Hinchliffe, B. in Elliott, B. (ed.) "Aspects of Barnsley 6."

[210] See Thomas, P. in Barnsley FHS Journal, Vol. 14, No. 2, April, 2006.

[211] Burland, op cit.

[212] Hobsbawn, E.J. "Labouring Men."

[213] Gilbert, op cit.

[214] Ibid.

[215] Barnsley Independent, 31 May, 1884, Barnsley Archives.

[216] Barnsley Independent, 17 September, 1892, Barnsley Archives.

# Descent into Silence

Barnsley Chronicle, 22 January, 1876, quoted in Polehampton, H., op cit.

[218] Email to author.

[219] Machin, op cit.

[220] Wain, K. "The Coal Mining Industry of Barnsley, Rotherham and Worksop."

[221] Lake, F. and Preece, R. "Voices From The Dark."

[222] See Griffin, A.R. "The Collier."

[223] Machin, op cit.

[224] Barnsley Independent, 31 May, 1884, Barnsley Archives.

[225] Fisher, P.J. "The Politics of Sudden Death."

[226] Baines, E. "Baines's Yorkshire," Vol.1.

[227] Burland, op cit.

[228] Sp. St. 60686.

[229] Barnsley Independent, 31 May, 1884, Barnsley Archives.

[230] Held by Heritage Silkstone.

[231] Ibid.

[232] Singleton, op cit.

[233] D148/4/2 1-5 and D148/5/2 1-2, West Yorkshire Archives.

[234] Tate, W.E. "The Parish Chest."

[235] Hey,1993, op cit.

[236] D148/5/2/2, West Yorkshire Archives.

[237] West Riding Quarter Sessions Order Books, West Yorkshire Archives.

[238] Quoted in Threlkeld, op cit.

[239] Tate, op cit.

[240] Ibid.

[241] West Riding Quarter Sessions Order Books, West Yorkshire Archives.

[242] Smith, D. "A Brief History of Methodism in Clowne." Internet source.

[243] Pratt, op cit.

[244] Ibid.

[245] British Coal Authority map no. 10322.

[246] Sp. St. 60609/5.

[247] Sp. St. 60579/23.

[248] Sp. St. 60609/5.

[249] See Sp. St. 60609/19/21/22/29/31/35/37.

[250] Goodchild, 1986, op cit.

[251] Ibid.

[252] Sp. St. 60684.

[253] Keir MSS, John Goodchild Collection, West Yorkshire Archives.

[254] Sp. St. 60684/5.

[255] Sp. St. 60657/7.

[256] Sp. St. 60609/19/21.

[257] Sp. St. 60609/22/29/31.

[258] Sp. St. 60684/5.

[259] Polehampton, op cit.

[260] Nixon, G. "Hidden Art On Your Doorstep" research file.

[261] Ibid.

[262] Ibid.

[263] See Elliott, B. "The Making of Barnsley."

[264] Barnsley Independent, 31 May, 1884, Barnsley Archives.

[265] Burt, T. "An Autobiography."

266 Email to author, 16 September, 2020.

267 Barnsley Independent, 31 May, 1884, Barnsley Archives.

268 West Riding Quarter Sessions Order Books, West Yorkshire Archives.

269 Tate, op cit.

270 Singleton, op cit.

271 Sp. St. 60657/3-7.

272 Sp..St. 60718.

273 Stirling, A.M.W. "Life's Little Day."

274 West Riding Quarter Sessions Order Books, West Yorkshire Archives.

275 Elliott, B., 2006.

276 Sheffield Independent, 17 September, 1892. Sheffield Archives.

277 Barnsley Chronicle, 31 December, 1892, Barnsley Archives.

278 Goodchild, 1986, op cit.

279 Pratt, op cit.

280 Ibid.

281 Sp. St. 60657/7.

282 Ibid.

283 Tate, op cit.

284 Morton, op cit.

285 Sp. St. 60684/10.

286 Sp. St. 60609/5.

287 See www.ashton-under-lyne.com/information/map04.btm

288 DYD 746258.

289 Smith, W. "Morley Ancient and Modern."

290 See www.closedpubs.co.uk/yorkshire/morley

291 Jackson, B., op cit.

292 Walvin, J. H. in Hargreaves and Haigh, op cit.

293 Ibid.

294 Machin, op cit.

295 Threlkeld, op cit.

296 B940, Barnsley Archives.

297 Elliott, 2006, op cit.

298 B940, Barnsley Archives.

299 The manuscript of mining engineer, G.H. Teasedale, suggesting these requirements is noted in Elliott, 2006, op cit.

300 Thorp, W. "On the causes of the explosions in the Barnsley or Thick Coal of Yorkshire."

301 Machin, op cit.

302 Turton, K. "A Grim Almanac of South Yorkshire."

303 Threlkeld, op cit.

304 Machin, op cit.

305 Ibid.

306 I am particularly grateful to Jane Raistrick, of Heritage Silkstone, for pointing out this connection.

# Acknowledgements

MY INTEREST in the Norcroft tragedy goes back very many years and my research into it, and the writing of this book, has involved the support and help of very many people to whom I am most grateful.

My wife Julia and children Robert and Rebecca have been wonderfully supportive throughout. Fortunately, Julia shares my passion for history but also has some excellent computer skills which I have had to rely upon on a regular basis. In addition, her research expertise has been crucial in uncovering some of the material used in the book. It is quite remarkable that our two families, from considerable distances apart, had direct ancestors living in the Cawthorne area at exactly the same time during the nineteenth century, both with connections to Norcroft.

I am especially grateful to Scratching Shed for their willingness to publish the book and have particularly appreciated all Phil Caplan's advice and support during its completion. The resources of the National Coal Mining Museum for England have helped with my research and I have appreciated the interest in the book shown by colleagues at the Museum.

Members of the Norcroft Memorial Committee have been central to this story being written. I am reluctant to single any of them out in particular but genuinely doubt that the completion of the book, and the earlier erection of the disaster memorial, would have happened without the interest, enthusiasm and passion of Steve Wyatt. His commitment to mining history has been central to the exploration of the Norcroft story, and his own research has been of immense help to me. Steve's wife Christine and son Derrick have also given great support.

David Flack's lifetime in coal mining has been fundamental to the Committee's work, in both establishing the likely location of the shaft involved and understanding the detailed circumstances of the accident. I am most grateful to him for his interpretation of some of the underground maps and surface plans from the time of the accident and allowing me to include his explanation of the likely haulage arrangements of the period within the book.

Geoff Wake has given great leadership over several years as the Memorial Committee's Chair and his local knowledge of the Cawthorne and Silkstone areas has been of a source of great help. Similarly, I am greatly indebted to Geoff Mosley for sharing his detailed memories of the recent history of Norcroft and to his wife Enid and daughter Catherine Wood for their commitment to the Norcroft Memorial project. Jim Ritchie has had a longstanding interest in the industrial history of the area and I very much appreciate him allowing me to tap into his very detailed knowledge of the links with the Silkstone wagonway which were fundamental to the operation of the Banks Estate pits. Rosemary Preece's experience from her past work at the National Coal Mining Museum has been particularly helpful in understanding the employment of children at the time, about which she has herself written. Peter Kilner and Keith Bratley, from the Cawthorne Silver Jubilee Museum, have both been very supportive and their local knowledge has been invaluable. Most regrettably, John Lees an active member of the Committee since its formation, passed away some time before this book's completion but his advice during its writing was of great assistance.

Chris Walley, who lives at Upper Norcroft, has always been most helpful when I and others have made unannounced visits or I have made phone calls asking for information. I am most grateful to her and her family for sharing their photographs of the cottages. I am similarly obliged to Chris Nixon for allowing the use of a photograph from his personal collection. Ruth Sheard has been wonderfully supportive in helping me with some of the proverbial brick walls I have encountered in working through many of the old records of the area, and Brian Elliott has been a constant source of advice and encouragement. His numerous publications on the local history of the area over very many years have been most useful in offering important background information and I very much appreciate him writing the foreword to the book. Barry Jackson's insights into Cawthorne's history have been of great help and I have been grateful for his personal advice on sources of information. Lisa Dalton has given both advice and help with reproducing old photographs and paintings, and Harry Malkin's illustration of the Norcroft shaft ascent has been helpful in understanding the accident's circumstances. I have also particularly appreciated the support of Jane and David

Raistrick of Heritage Silkstone and of Gerry Wright, who lectures in nineteenth century history at the U3A. They have introduced me to sources I would not otherwise have found, for which I am most grateful.

I have spent a considerable amount of time in Barnsley Archives and Local Studies and the staff there have been outstandingly helpful. Barnsley Council have given a great deal of priority to preserving the area's local history and this is reflected in the commitment and expertise of those working in this section of the local authority. I am especially grateful to Gillian Nixon, an archivist at Barnsley over many years, for her personal interest in the book and the loan of items from her own research into the Thorp and Fox families in connection with the Art on Your Doorstep project. Through her, I have been fortunate to have contact with Hugh Polehampton, a direct descendant of Samuel Thorp the Norcroft coalmaster, and I have appreciated him passing on information from his own research into his ancestors and their connections to the Fox family. West Yorkshire History Centre and Sheffield Archives have given excellent advice and assistance, and the Leeds Anglican Diocesan Office have also been of help.

I would like to acknowledge, in particular, my use of publications produced by both the Barnsley Family History Society and the Huddersfield Family History Society which have been invaluable in writing the book. I have appreciated the interest of my cousin Anne Wilkinson in this research and her longstanding personal encouragement of my study of our family history. Her unique summing up of the consequence of genealogy will always stay with me: "...they seem so clear, and so close – but so gone." My cousins, Mike Dunn and Peter Hinchliffe, have also supported my research.

Finally, it is sad to have to place on record my

particular appreciation for past help received from several people who are no longer alive. John Goodchild, the former Wakefield archivist, gave me the initial steer with this research many years back and his Collection held at the West Yorkshire History Centre contains a vast amount of material relevant to any study of the Cawthorne and Silkstone areas. Professor Malcolm Chase at Leeds University was a constructive critic when I first did some formal research on Norcroft.

This research and the eventual book was the direct consequence of a passion for local history inspired by the renowned Yorkshire historians, Dr. George Redmonds and professor David Hey. I shall forever be in their debt for enthusing me about a subject which left me totally unmoved during my school years. I regard it as a great privilege to have known both of them.

Above all, I am indebted to 'Auntie' May Ellis for opening the door which led to what, for me, has been a compelling investigation of our quite recent past.

# Lineage of John to David Hinchliffe

JEHOSHAPHAT HINCHLIFFE = MARY WILCOCK
*(Great, Great Grandparents)*

Possible parents of John Hinchliffe

BENJAMIN HINCHLIFFE = ELIZA TEAL PAVER
*(Great Grandparents)*

OLIVER HINCHLIFFE = ETHEL WOODHEAD
*(Grandparents)*

ROBERT VICTOR HINCHLIFFE = MURIEL PRESTON
*(Parents)*

DAVID MARTIN HINCHLIFFE = JULIA NORTH

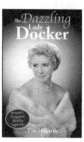

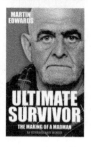

Investigate our other titles and
stay up to date with all our latest releases at
www.scratchingshedpublishing.co.uk